MW00474551

# BEING THE BODY OF CHRIST

MARCI ALBORGHETTI

# BEING
# THE BODY
# OF CHRIST

### What the People of the Passion
### teach us about Jesus today

TWENTY
THIRD 2317
PUBLICATIONS
NEW LONDON, CT 06320
WWW.23RDPUBLICATIONS.COM

TWENTY-THIRD PUBLICATIONS
A Division of Bayard
One Montauk Avenue, Suite 200
New London, CT 06320
(860) 437-3012 or (800) 321-0411
www.23rdpublications.com

Copyright ©2012 Marci Alborghetti. All rights reserved. No part of
this publication may be reproduced in any manner without prior written permission of the publisher. Write to the Permissions Editor.

ISBN: 978-1-58595-892-4
Library of Congress Control Number: 2012953104
Printed in the U.S.A.

# DEDICATION

*For God*
*To Charlie*

# CONTENTS

# INTRODUCTION

WHEN CHRISTIANS SPEAK OF THE BODY OF CHRIST they often think, first, of the Holy Eucharist, a blessing and sacrament that we receive, the gift of Christ himself to nourish our faith and strengthen our worship communities. "Do this in remembrance of me," Jesus told the apostles, and so we do whenever we receive this Spirit-saturated gift.

But as Saint Paul told us, we are also the body of Christ, and each of us is a part of it (1 Corinthians 12:27). What does this mean for us? How are we joined in and to the Eucharist? How can we become an active part of Jesus? How are we to become Jesus' eyes and ears, feet and hands, arms and legs, heart and mouth and voice in the world today? How are we to become so intimately connected to Jesus that we move from passive, though mentally engaged, followers to active, physical disciples?

Can we *embody* the teachings of Jesus?

Those who loved and believed in Jesus enough to remain with him on Good Friday did just that. In their physical connection to Jesus they model for us a commitment that we can discern and renew in ourselves. They received Jesus' body on Good Friday, not as the Holy Eucharist, but in all its tortured and torn and broken physicality. They witnessed the damage done in the preceding 18 hours, as well as the wear and tear from three hard years spent on the road securing their—and our—salvation. They took into their arms a body that had *worked* long and hard before it had been abused and crucified. In serving the physical Jesus in this lifeless, wounded form, they were able to bear piercing witness to what and who Jesus had been. Without yet knowing what this death would achieve, they were as physically bound to Jesus in death as they had been in life and would soon be in and through his resurrection.

These are the people who can become our guides as we seek to commit ourselves physically, emotionally, and spiritually to Jesus and his teachings. In these pages we experience Mary's anguish and vivid memories as she holds her son's cold, bruised body in her arms and recalls the hope and excitement she'd felt rocking the warm newborn decades before; John's sorrow at this apparent ugly ending and his determination to honor the One who'd taken him by the hand and pulled him out of his fishing boat three years earlier; Mary Magdalene's terrible grief and humility as she tenderly wipes away the blood and filth from the feet she once washed with her tears and dried with her hair; Nicodemus' regret at having been unable to stop this travesty and his wonder at the brilliance of the Rabbi he met in secret; Salome's strength in preparing the body and her fear that what she'd asked Jesus for her own sons would, indeed, come to pass; Joseph of Arimathea's courage in seeking Jesus' body and his realization that his own future now belonged to God; the Roman centurion's comprehension of the terrible mistake made by the empire he served and his transformation from enemy to disciple.

Each of these had received Jesus in his or her own way during life, and each physically received his body on that bleak day of death, just as each would rejoice in his resurrection. In devoting themselves to Jesus' body that day, their part in the body of Christ became irrevocable. They would go on to use and, in some cases, sacrifice their own bodies in serving the risen Jesus by bringing the message of Christianity to their world. In witnessing their commitment and the joy they experienced in the resurrection, we too can experience the kind of profound transformation that will enable us to become the body of Christ in ours.

As a reader you will bring your own experience to these stories. You may wish to first read the story through, letting yourself enter into the experiences of the person speaking. Then, go back and read it again, allowing yourself to pause and consider any phrase, sentence, or portion of the story that strikes you. Stop and reflect on this before going on. Ask yourself: how am I like this person? When have I felt like this? What does this experience mean for the way I approach Christ? For the way I pray? For the way I live my life? After you have absorbed the story to the fullest possible extent, move on to the prayer, the questions, and the action suggestions. It is often helpful to gather with others to talk about what the story means to you, to pray together, and to discuss the questions and actions at the end of each chapter. Feel free to explore other thoughts and feelings that you experience in reading and reflecting on the stories.

*For where two or three are gathered in my name, I am there in their midst.*

MATTHEW 18:20

.......................................................................................................

*But you do not belong to the world, because I have chosen you out of the world.* JOHN 15:19

.......................................................................................................

*I pray not only on behalf of these, but also for those who through their word will come to believe in me. May they all be one. As you, Father, are in me and I in you, may they also be in us so that the world may believe that you have sent me.*

JOHN 17:20-21

.......................................................................................................

*For you will not abandon me to the netherworld nor allow your holy one to suffer corruption.* ACTS 2:27

# One

# MARY, MOTHER *of* JESUS

*There, ahead of them, went the star that they had seen at its rising, until it stopped over the place where the Child was...they were overwhelmed with joy.* MATTHEW 2:9-10

WHEN I SAW MY SON DIE, I FELT NOTHING BUT RELIEF. It flooded through me in waves. The bitter-sweet release. What else could I feel? I'd watched my child struggle to breathe for more than six hours, every breath a battle witnessed in a heaving chest, a closing throat, a body quivering with pain and exhaustion. The truth is I *prayed* for Jesus to die. I know that his Father heard my prayer for release as I watched my son die.

My relief was short-lived, followed swiftly—not by the guilt you might think a mother would feel upon praying for her son's death—by complete numbness. I was dead to all feeling. I understood the reality: that after almost a full day of constant torture and humiliation, my child had died, gone to the Father who'd given him to me over thirty years ago. I comprehended this. And also that Jesus' friends and brothers and sisters—many of whom were already in hiding—were threatened with suffering the same fate. Yes, I knew that even I was in danger, no less than those who surround me now in this dark, bleak hour before twilight. We might be hunted by those who'd killed my son. Though I knew all this to be true, I felt nothing.

Now I hear my friends all around me, the murmurs of worry in the midst of their own weeping and fear. I can smell their fear: John and Magdalene, Salome and Nicodemus, Joseph and even the awe-struck centurion who'd stood with increasing discomfort by the cross. It is like the smell just before a violent storm, and it had come with the black clouds and rain that poured down when Jesus died. It had come with that driving torrent, and now it clings to all of them, their clothes, their cold sweat, their tears: the smell of dread, for what had been and for what is to come.

I understand that there is goodness in them all, for in the midst of their horror, they are worried about me. I do not share their concern, do not wish to, but I know they feel it. John, helping them take the body down, is casting quick, furtive glances at me. The poor boy! To be saddled with another mother at this, the most terrifying and chaotic moment in his young life. He hadn't expected that, of all things, when Jesus spoke to him from the cross. I could tell he was disappointed when Jesus finally managed to form the words through cracked and bleeding lips. When John had realized that Jesus was trying to speak to him, he surged forward, as close as the centurion would let him come, desperate to hear every word. I saw him try to hold Jesus' gaze, but my son's eyes were crusted with sweat and tears and blood, with only a glimmer of light visible.

Still, John leaned forward, grimly determined to hear what

his teacher would have him do now. I could see both the fear and hope in the young man's face. None of the other disciples had followed Jesus to this cross; John knew that. He alone would be the one to receive the final message; he alone would have the responsibility and the honor of conveying Jesus' last words and instructions to the others. I could see, too, that John hoped for something extraordinary from Jesus. It was said by the other apostles, with not a little envy, that John was the most loved, and I think that, within himself, he believed this to be true. It was natural that he would look for a word or two that might reflect that.

What John got was both more and less than he'd hoped for. *"Here is your mother."* [John 19:27]

Poor John! It was an assignment of love without any word of love. It was a burden of love without any chance for honor or renown. Jesus didn't even call him by name. Then, without warning, another mother to care for! As if Salome wasn't enough, maybe too much, to cope with in and of herself. Brash and strong, she had with her own voice many times over earned her title as the mother of the sons of thunder. But John needn't worry. I will be no trouble. Perhaps God will grant me another prayer today and let me die with my son.

And what of Salome, John's true mother? Did she hear Jesus' words to John? She gave no sign of it, though I doubt she would have even if she'd heard. She loves me, I know, but not as much as she loved Jesus. So strong, so practical, so able to do what I cannot seem to do now. Salome is in constant motion and has been throughout this day of devastation. She paced back and forth under the cross, wearing a path in the dirt and then the mud when the heavens opened and sent the downpour. She gives constant voice to what she feels, as she always has, first maligning the centurion and his cohort, next muttering imprecations against the Sanhedrin, then, when she could not keep herself from gazing up at Jesus writhing in torment, wailing in helpless sorrow and rage. She tore at her clothes and beat her hands against her own head and chest. All day long she's been like this, but now she's grown quiet. She still moves slowly back and forth among us, going from one to the other, trying to understand what is to be done, trailing a gentle hand along my shoulders or upon my head as she passes me. It is true: as much as anyone here can understand me, Salome, a mother herself, does.

Magdalene has no child, and she kneels beside me now in the muck, wanting to help the others with Jesus' body, but unwilling to leave my side. It is ever thus with her, always in some sort of conflict within herself. One could never know what might be troubling her, and because she's grown accustomed over the years to being an outcast, she keeps her struggles to herself. Still, they are always written on her face and in her eyes, these battles and uncertainties that pulled her this way and that. The only time I ever truly saw her at peace was in Jesus' presence. She didn't seem to find it necessary that he speak to her in those moments, and truly, she seldom spoke to him at all. Simply being near Jesus soothed her; and though it did for most people, Magdalene was different. What she felt for my son, what she received from him, was beyond words. Even I couldn't fully comprehend their bond. He said nothing to Magdalene this day before dying, had not directed any of those few cryptic words to her, and yet she kept her eyes upon him. No matter the wracking pain she witnessed, no matter how rattling and choking the breath she heard, her gaze had not wavered. I believe she did not want to let him down. And she didn't.

Nicodemus carries his regret like a crushing burden upon his shoulders. He is not a young man, he is even older than I, but he has aged another lifetime in these past hours. I see him now, shaking his head in dismay and disbelief, carefully cradling the heavy weight of aloes he brought, as they take the body from the cross. Nicodemus blames himself; I know this. He believes that he could have done something to stop his fellow Pharisees, his brothers in the Sanhedrin, from condemning Jesus. He shouldn't punish himself. Though I don't fully understand how my son came to this place, I know that this grief-stricken, old Pharisee could have done nothing to prevent this end. I wish he could know how much Jesus had looked forward to their conversations. Many nights after Nicodemus had gone home, Jesus told me how much he enjoyed confounding and debating with the good-hearted, curious elder. I know I should summon the strength to share these memories with Nicodemus, for this would comfort him. But I cannot. Where is my heart?

There is much I could also tell Joseph, the other secret disciple who came from Arimathea to converse with Jesus many times over the past three years. Unlike my Joseph, this Joseph was a rich, powerful man, another member of the Sanhedrin who was unable in the end to influence them in Jesus' favor. For all of Joseph's wealth and power, and even his thoughtless arrogance with his colleagues, he was strangely gentle and humble when it came to Jesus. Had my son brought this out in the large and otherwise self-important man? Perhaps, but I know that Jesus reacted to something in this Joseph in much the same way he'd reacted to my Joseph, the man who'd guided him through childhood and into manhood. Was it the shared name? Was it that Joseph of Arimathea resembled my husband? He did, fleetingly, though it was hard to imagine my dear, quiet, shabbily dressed husband in the fine clothes of this bold, strong man.

But Jesus had seen it, and I believe it allowed the two un-likeliest of strangers to become fast friends. They would talk through the night, and once or twice after Joseph had left us, Jesus would ask me if the Arimathean reminded me of our own Joseph. He would peer at me and pester me, demanding an answer. Finally, I would allow, "There is some resemblance, but no one reminds me of father. For me there is no one like him." I could tell that did not satisfy my son, but Jesus knew better than to push me on the subject. He'd seen how long it had taken me to recover from Joseph's death. I wondered now, had Jesus considered how long it would take me to recover from his? Or whether I ever would at all? Is he about to call me to him, knowing it is all I have left to want?

It occurs to me that I should despise this centurion who stays with us even now, long after his cohort has returned to the Roman barracks. Still, other than a mild, distant curiosity, I feel nothing toward him at all. He had no real role in this. He's done what he'd been commanded to do; yet I've seen him over the day grow more and more disturbed as he guarded the cross, presumably to keep us from helping Jesus, but in those last hours, he let us come as close as we wished. He'd allowed John to come within an arm's length when Jesus wanted to speak to him. In that final hour the centurion appeared confused, as if he'd begun to think his role was more to protect than to guard Jesus. When a mocking onlooker broke through and made to spit upon my son, the centurion dealt him a blow that sent him spinning back to the jeering mob. After Salome took note of that, she'd stopped harassing the centurion, though even now, as he stands uncertainly among us—an outsider who has no place here—she sends suspicious glances his way.

I sit in benumbed silence watching them all. I don't know what to do next; I don't care. What could it matter? As Jesus said, it is over. My life, the whole purpose of me, died on that cross, and I too am dead to everything around me, dead to my own life. I sink down in the mud, some of it mixed with Jesus' blood, and stay there, barely conscious of the cold damp soaking through my clothes, clinging wetly to my skin.

It comes into my mind that Jesus would have teased me for this—I, always so determined to keep a clean home and wear fresh clothes no matter how many times we moved, no matter how much time we spent on the road for fear or in the quest to teach. He would have laughingly chided me, and, yes, there would have been a touch of worry. I imagine his words: "Mother, what are you doing? You say *I* have no concern for clothes or a clean sleeping place? Look at you, resting there in the mud! It will take you hours to clean your clothes. Come now, get up." And then my son would have lifted me up and led me to shelter, never letting go of me.

But Jesus does not tease me or chide me or lift me up and lead me to safety. I close my eyes and wait for him to come, but he does not. Whatever emotion was left in me drains into the mud.

Now they come to me and place him in my arms. I feel them gently lower the weight of the body. I will not open my eyes. What are they doing? Do they believe that I want this? Do I?

His body settles and I automatically lift my arms to support it. I would have not thought it possible, but the body is colder and wetter than mine, except that mine is a shivering, clinging, living cold. His is a smooth, finished cold.

It cannot be my Boy. I will not look. I close my eyes tighter and start to rock back and forth a little. I hear a high, thin, keening cry. Mine. And then, his.

*Except not this body's, but my baby boy's cry.* I urge Joseph to give the screeching newborn to me, and though my good husband is fearful of how weak the birth has left me, he complies, putting Jesus into my arms. Not cold and still now; no, warm and wriggling and quieting at the touch of my hands and skin. I know Joseph is smiling down at us, but I have eyes for nothing but my son. This tiny miracle in so many ways.

How many times in the past nine months had I been confused, uncertain, wondering? How many times had I fought feelings of regret for the childhood God had seen fit to take from me so swiftly and irretrievably? How frequently had I seen my mother and father gaze at me with anxious bewilderment, and the villagers with something much harsher? How often had I glanced from under my lashes at Joseph and wondered, "Can he...? Will he...? Why would he...?" In the end, I had drawn strength from his certainty and determination, especially after the dream.

Now, this. My infant seems to know me already and grows calmer in my arms. I am no longer afraid, no longer confused about the future. It is not that I know what will come next; I don't know what will happen tomorrow. But I am no longer worried about it. I feel that my child and I belong to a greater world and, at the same time, a world of just we two. I believe us to be safe. After all, look what God has done! The Messiah. Oh yes, but *my* son of *my* body. What could be wrong in our world?

For as long as I can, I will close my eyes to the signs, cling to the belief that all will be well. *Normal.* I start this very night as I hold Jesus, watching the tiny hands wave and the perfect feet kick in the air. While I wrap my newborn tightly as my mother had shown me before we left Nazareth, I am conscious of a sudden tension in Joseph. I look up and then follow his gaze to see the ragged, half-naked band of shepherds hesitating at the mouth of the cave. It must be an unusually clear night, I think, for the light behind them to be so strong. Ignoring my husband's distrust, his tightening grip on his staff, I motion them in; I have a son for them to gaze upon! Does every mother feel that hers is the first baby to be born on the earth? Why shouldn't we celebrate? I ask Joseph gaily with my silent look of exultation. His face softens, and we welcome the shepherds in.

They gaze at my boy in what seems to me to be awe and astonishment as they share with us the broken bits and pieces of food that is their only meal. It may be a poor repast, but we have not eaten in some time, and I am happy to see Joseph take some food. Do I listen to what the shepherds tell us? About the vision of angels and their declaration of the prophecy fulfilled? Well, yes. But what of it? It is no surprise to me, of all people, that Jesus is special, a gift from God. Why should that inspire such apparent fear in them? What is it in their words that makes Joseph's eyes darken and the frown shadow his features? What could there possibly be to fear?

As time passes, it becomes more difficult to ignore the prophet and prophetess in the temple when we present our infant son after the prescribed time in the manner of our people. For any parents of a firstborn boy, this is a joyous day, the day we dedicate our son to God. For us, knowing Jesus has come directly from God, it is even more extraordinary. I see in Joseph's eyes some trepidation. He wonders if our experience of this day will be different from those of countless other parents since the days of Moses. I will not question him about this, because I do not want to share his anxiety. I will not allow myself to acknowledge that this ritual, in which we "give" our son to God, is more real for us than it has been for any other Hebrew couple. Aren't we simply offering the gifts to "redeem" Jesus just as other parents have? Won't we walk out of this temple with our baby, the same way we had walked in? I avoid any thought that we are "giving" a child who would never really be ours to give, that the firstborn son we offer is being offered for the world.

He is my son. How can I feel otherwise? I cannot know what is to come. And so as we leave the temple, when Simeon comes upon us and takes Jesus from Joseph's arms, I refuse to be startled or distressed. After all, who could resist admiring such a beautiful boy? Even when Simeon speaks of his eyes having seen God's salvation, I smile, as if in kindness to an addled old man, and I do not meet Joseph's fearful glance as Simeon blesses us, the parents. This is not so unusual, is it, to bless the proud parents of a newborn son? But Simeon is not finished. As though determined to make himself understood to me, he looks directly at me, capturing and holding my wandering gaze.

*"And a sword will pierce your own soul, too."*

I snatch Jesus from his arms and swiftly turn to leave the temple, Joseph hurriedly following. I will not let this day be spoiled. This is *our* day, our first public day as a family. I barely hear the prophetess, Anna, echoing the words of the old man, and I will not heed those watching us closely, curiously now, after all this attention. Jesus does not belong to them. Holding my son close in my arms, I flee.

When the magi from the Orient come one night, I am calmer and long recovered from the birth, more the dutiful daughter and wife my mother has raised. Wondering at their appearance and purpose, Joseph nonetheless leads them into the small, humble place where we are staying. I can tell that Joseph is discomfited by this show of foreign power and wealth. What little we have, he has worked for, and worked hard with his hands and whole body. These three men have never worked with their bodies for anything. That is evident by the number of servants waiting outside, blocking the path and making no small commotion among the people of Bethlehem.

The three men enter alone, leaving their caravan outside. I can see that Joseph is ashamed to have no sturdy chairs or fine table, made with his own hands and laid with a good meal prepared by mine, to offer them. We are strangers here; everything we have was lent to us or purchased. Though I do not like to see my husband embarrassed, I do not share his discomfort. I am excited to see these men. I know, even before they speak of their long journey and the extraordinary star, that the treasure we have for them is far beyond anything they could offer us.

Am I proud? Yes.

Their gifts are magnificent. I have never seen gold, but I know from Joseph's widened eyes that the value of what the first man shows us is great. Frankincense I know from its use in worship, but I've never seen so much nor known the scent of any quite so exotic. But it is the man with the myrrh who, for a single moment, breaches the wall of well-being I've built around my son and me. For when he comes forward with his beautifully wrought container of the costly perfumed ointment used to both heal and anoint the dead, he, like his two companions, kneels before my child. But unlike them, he does not leave his gift by Jesus' crib. He comes to me, placing it at my feet, bowing. For an instant as he rises, my eyes meet his. They brim with sorrow and pity.

My heart and breath stops.

But I am swift in driving that flash of terror away. I make no
room for it; I will not allow it. Indeed, Joseph does not even
notice, and his eyes are always upon Jesus or me. When the
man who brought the myrrh turns finally to look sadly at me
as they leave, I smile coldly at him and deliberately move the
myrrh aside, pushing it toward the other gifts. I pretend to
take no note of the small, knowing smile he gave me in return.

*However, that is when I started to understand,* and,
though I buried that knowledge deep within myself, I've kept
that myrrh all these years. Before dawn today when the news
came that Jesus had been taken to Pilate, I put the jar of myrrh
in the sack I'd sewn into my robe. It had been there while I
waited in the dark for John and Salome and Mary to come for
me. It had been knocking against my body as we walked first
to Pilate's headquarters and then to this place of skulls. Tomorrow there will be a bruise where it had been beating against me
as we walked. Good.

What excuse can I give for my deliberate blindness in those
long-ago days? I was young? Yes. Of course. There was something more, though. I believe now that the Father was helping
me, allowing me to be willfully ignorant of what was to come.
Of this. How else could I have survived?

I open my eyes and gaze upon the pale, rain-washed body.
Reaching into the folds of my robe, I bring out the jar and
break the seal. Nicodemus has brought 100 pounds of aloes
with myrrh. But this is mine, laid at my feet.

# REFLECTING *on the* STORY

Our children will not die for the sake of Christianity. Chances are they will not suffer great bodily, or even emotional, pain for their faith. As parents we will not experience anything remotely like Mary's emotions as she came to understand what Jesus was really born to accomplish. No matter how many decades of the rosary we say or Stations of the Cross we complete, we cannot, truly, stand under the cross with her and feel what she felt. It is also unlikely that we will have children who are called to extreme physical sacrifices like those made by some saints. With the possible exception of those who see young family members become missionaries in dangerous countries unfriendly to Christianity, we need not fear for their safety.

And that's a good thing. Right?

Or has the relative "comfortable Christianity" we enjoy allowed us to become complacent about our children? If it is easy to imagine Mary trying to protect Jesus and herself from the difficulties and dangers of pursuing God's work, how much easier is it for us to shield our children from that call, especially when that call requires more than we—or they—want to give? Absent a pressing need for them—or us—to make any dramatic sacrifice to follow Jesus, how do we encourage them to take their part in being the body of Christ? If, thank God, they need not become martyrs or selfless saints, does that mean they should make no sacrifice to do God's work?

As Christian adults it is part of our work to prepare our children to follow Jesus, even when that journey is an arduous one. And to follow Jesus in this world cannot help but be complicated and sometimes difficult. We live in a society where wealth, power, and status are valued, while the humility, poverty, and extreme selflessness that Jesus preached are generally not. Our children are programmed to compete, sometimes relentlessly, for grades, college admissions, sports teams, and jobs. Jesus taught us to help others as much as—if not before—we help ourselves. Our young people are surrounded by a culture that puts a premium on youth, health, success, and beauty. Jesus spent time with lepers, prisoners, prostitutes, and the impoverished.

It is not easy to ask our children to "go against" the standards that society and the media set for them, but in some ways that is what we are called to do. However, unless we model Christian behavior for our youth, we cannot expect them to adopt, or adapt to, such a way of life. In this, too, we can turn to Mary who, in the single gospel exchange between her and the adult Jesus, called upon her son to stretch beyond his comfort zone.

Any parent can envision the scene between Jesus and Mary at the wedding in Cana. Mary, ever watchful and concerned for the comfort of others, notices that the wedding hosts are running out of wine. Jesus is in another part of the room or hall, enjoying himself and partying with friends and relatives. Mary motions for him to come to her, apart from the crowd. Does Jesus roll his eyes while making his way toward her? Does he raise his eyebrows at her: *Ma, what?*

*They don't have enough wine,* she says briefly, knowing that he knows what to do and that he knows she knows he knows.

*So what? I'm having fun. I'm not ready for everyone to know yet. Not my problem.*

And then Mary gives her son "the look." You don't have to

be a parent to know the look; you only need to have been a child with a mother. She says nothing more to Jesus. Just the look. Then she tells the wedding servers to do whatever her son tells them.

It is the classic mother-child moment, and yet, at the wedding in Cana, Mary was a faithful mother in many ways. Faithful to God the Father for following her instinct that it was time for Jesus to publicly reveal himself by performing the miracle of changing water to wine. Faithful to God's message of love by pushing Jesus to do a kindness that he was not necessarily interested in doing at that moment. Faithful to Jesus by urging him to behave well.

But in her exchange with Jesus at the Cana wedding, Mary is also faithful to us in that she demonstrates Christian parenting: she gives her son to God and to God's work.

## PRAYER

*Mary, mother of God and our mother, I can't help but be thankful that my children and the children in my life will not have to suffer the way Jesus suffered. Help me, gracious Mary, not to let thankfulness turn into complacency. Show me how to give the children in my life the courage to act as the body of Christ in our time even when it means they may give up some of the things the world values. Give me the words to describe for them the rewards of participating in Jesus' resurrection. Help me to show them my own role in the body of Christ and to demonstrate the enthusiasm and energy and love for Jesus that will motivate them. Teach me to be an example for them of how much they will gain for the little they may lose. Amen.*

## PRAYERFULLY ASK YOURSELF

1. When have I hesitated to encourage the children in my life to be the body of Christ because I fear it will be difficult for them or cause them to "miss out" on other opportunities?

2. How do the children in my life know from my actions that I follow Jesus?

3. What do we, as parents of our children and/or as the children of our parents, feel about Mary's memories and grief? How do we identify with her?

## TAKE ACTION

Model Christianity for children. If you have children, volunteer at an activity that they participate in—anything from helping to coach a team to bringing cupcakes to the class party. If you don't have children, seek such an opportunity through your church, family, friends, or a local child-centered organization where you can help out. Whether you are a parent or a parent-helper, be conscious during your volunteer effort of behaving as Jesus' emissary in their world for as long as you are there. Let the children experience Jesus through you.

## Two

# JOHN, *the* BELOVED APOSTLE

*When Jesus saw his mother and the disciple whom he loved standing beside her, he said to his mother, "**Woman, here is your son.**" Then he said to the disciple, "**Here is your mother.**"* JOHN 19:26-27

I KNOW WHAT I MUST DO, BUT I'M NOT SURE I CAN. His blood has hardened around the nails, forming a crust that makes the flesh of his hands adhere to the nails. He will feel nothing, I know, when I wrench the nails free from the shredded flesh, and yet, I can't bring myself to do it.

I have to find the strength. I am the only one of the twelve who made this terrible vigil, and I feel both the burden of responsibility and of love. Was I the only one of us at the foot of the cross because I am the one my brothers call the beloved? Did Jesus love me more? I never saw a sign of that. He treated us all much the same. Did I love the Master more than they did? How can I make that judgment? Who can know what is in another person's heart? Or was it a sense of duty that overcame my terror of following Jesus on the road to Calvary? Was it my need to show my love by supporting Mary, his mother, and now mine?

I don't have an answer to even one of these questions. I don't know my own mind anymore. I had given my mind and my will and my body to Jesus for direction; now what am I to do? What is my work? Where is my will? I only know that I could not help myself, I could not keep myself from joining Mary and Salome, my own mother, and the other women who followed right to the foot of the cross. I did such a seemingly rash and courageous thing without hesitation, but now that Jesus is gone, I cannot even bring myself to take the nails from his poor hands.

I bow my head and think of the last day and night. How could it have gone so wrong? How could we have started with that glorious Passover feast, only to end with this torn and broken body we now take from this cross? James, my brother, warned us. He saw it coming. He is the practical one. He understood the risks that Jesus was taking. Even last night, in the joy of that festival and of Jesus speaking to us so clearly, James was worried. I saw him scowling when Jesus washed our feet, fearful when the Lord gave us the bread and wine. But I don't think even James knew how fast it would come, how swiftly everything would be taken from us, how rapidly we would lose control of our lives, of our Master.

Even after Jesus was taken in Gethsemane, after I'd followed at a distance into the very courtyard of the high priest, I still didn't fully understand. Something would happen to stop this travesty, I'd thought. Jesus would speak so eloquently and brilliantly in his own defense that the Sanhedrin would release him, and perhaps even some of them would come over to us in the process. What a wondrous miracle that would be! We Jews would then bring the kingdom of God to the world! Or perhaps Abba, the Father, would intervene to save Jesus and show the leaders of his people that Jesus was, indeed, his Messiah. I even allowed myself to imagine that Pilate, our enemy, might be transformed and decide to release Jesus instead of Barabbas.

At every step of the way, from Gethsemane to Golgotha, everything went wrong. Nothing happened as I'd hoped and prayed. I felt like I was living in a fever dream, something impossible to imagine, something that couldn't be true. As I watched Jesus stumbling and falling along the rough, stone-covered way to Golgotha, I must have been numb. My mind closed down. Everything moved slowly, like I was seeing through someone else's eyes. It was not until they stretched his arms out upon the wood and drove the nails into his flesh, and I heard the single, unwilling, piercing scream of pain, that I fully wakened to what was happening. And I knew, as my friend and Lord's anguished cry echoed in the sudden silence of the Place of Skulls, that whatever and whoever else Jesus was, he was a man.

Now I sense them around me, watching, waiting. I feel their sorrow and sympathy. I feel the weight of their pity, for they know I have taken on this task. I have claimed it for myself. As a punishment? It may be; I don't know. Could I be any more punished than to have witnessed what I've witnessed? To have lost what I have lost? I feel Salome's stricken gaze upon me; only the one who gave birth to me could fully understand what I feel right now, yet I'm not even sure that she, in her wild and angry grief, can know my searing pain and disappointment.

How does *she* feel? What was it like for her to hear Jesus, hanging in agony on the cross, make Mary my mother, my responsibility? I did not dare to look at Salome in those moments and can only wonder how she reacted. Or *if* she reacted, for she has grown accustomed to subjecting her considerable will to the will and words of Jesus. She had come to surrender herself to the Master's word more than she ever had to my father's. She would have known, even before Jesus finished uttering those few instructions, that it was done. For me, from then on, Mary would come first. It could be no other way. It was the only thing I had left to give my Lord, and I would give it. Salome had become, in that instant, entirely the responsibility of James. She would have known that, and how she feels about it may be something I will never know.

The question I do not want to ask is of myself. How did I feel when Jesus spoke to me? The absolute truth, which no one but me will ever know, makes me ashamed. I felt hurt. Yes, with all that my Master was suffering, I was selfish enough to feel my own childish hurt! It wasn't that I didn't want to care for Mary, to make her my mother according to the customs of our people. I was honored, if a little uncertain as to how I would carry out such an overwhelming requirement. After all, I had given up my livelihood, my fishing boat, my family heritage. I suppose I could take it back up again, beg my father to take me back and let me earn my living and the keeping of Mary as best as I can. Yes, that might work. I will talk to James about it. I cannot keep any thought for the future long in my mind. How can there be a future at all, now?

What dismayed me as I listened from the foot of the cross was that these were Jesus' only words to me. It is hard for me to make this shameful admission even to myself, but it's true: I hoped for more. Indeed, for a fleeting moment, I thought I deserved more! Was I not called the beloved disciple? Had I not shown bravery that was lacking in the others by following

Jesus all the way to Golgotha? Was I not protecting Mary with my own body and holding her as she swayed in sorrow and heartrending grief?

I thought to myself, could Jesus not have given me something more? Something to hold onto in the dark days to come? Something to share with my brothers and the other believers that would comfort them, and yes, perhaps even demonstrate my loyalty in that he had chosen me as messenger, even leader? Something, anything, to help me understand how this could have happened?

Now, the very memory of my selfishness fills me with remorse. How could I have been thinking of myself, my honor, my position, my pain, when Jesus was suffering so desperately? It was as though in that one moment when I realized Jesus meant to speak to me, I forgot all that he'd taught me about humility, unselfishness, love. And now I am an empty vessel, purged even of myself; all arrogance and strength and certainty have been leeched out of me. There is no service left for me to give Jesus. There is nothing I can do to show my sorrow, to earn my forgiveness, for I know now that forgiveness cannot be earned. The body here before me is testimony to that, for how could any among men and women "earn" this sacrifice?

There is one thing left for me to do, though he will not know it, and I am ready to do it now. I use the wedge the centurion has silently given me and wrench out one nail, and then, the other. His hands fall and, instinctively, I reach out and catch them. As the cold, torn hands fall into my grasp, I close my eyes and remember.

*I'd first noticed those hands three years ago* when Jesus sat, uninvited, in our fishing boat and began to help

James and me mend our nets. Our father, Zebedee, was busy with the day's catch, bargaining with the buyers, and didn't even notice that Jesus had come onto the boat. To this day, I believe my father regrets not seeing Jesus at first and driving him away. Zebedee lost us in those unguarded moments, and he has never gotten us back.

James and I were curious about this stranger, but tired from long hours fishing, and so we said nothing at first. Our neighbors Simon and Andrew had followed Jesus from their boat to ours, so James and I thought he might be seeking work on one of our vessels. Upon occasion, we shared the hired men so that everyone would have enough work. But when I glanced over at Simon, usually so forward and boisterous, he said nothing. His eyes, and Andrew's, were fixed on the stranger.

But Jesus did not ask for work or even speak at first, instead sitting beside us and working silently on the nets. He was not adept at mending nets; we could see it wasn't familiar work, yet he seemed to improve at the task even as we watched. James and I exchanged glances, but still we said nothing. It was then that I noticed Jesus' hands. Though he was not large or powerful-looking, his hands were strong and agile. They bore the hardened calluses of a man who worked for a living, but there was a difference here that I couldn't name. He was not like us or our hired men. There was something else that struck me then as strange, and that made me feel a little uncomfortable with myself: I did not want him to leave us.

And so I was the first to speak. "Friend, I think that repairing nets is not familiar work. Your hands and skill, though, tell us that you are no stranger to hard work."

He merely smiled and kept on with the nets, getting better and better at it by the moment. We were almost finished, and my fear grew that Jesus would disappear when the last tear was mended. I could see from the bemusement on James' face that he felt the same. The silence stretched on, and finally, Jesus said that he was carpenter by trade.

His voice did nothing to lessen our curiosity or the inexplicable attraction we both felt. Although it was a Gallilean dialect like ours, there was a beauty and richness to the voice that, again, made me wonder where he was from and what his purpose could be. James found the courage to ask, "You have no carpentry work at present? You want to hire on to fish?"

He smiled in the same way, a way I can only describe as mysterious and even a little amused. After a moment Jesus told James that both builders and fishermen had their places in God's kingdom.

James looked at me and raised his eyebrows, but I was suddenly shy and did not want to question this peculiar statement. James, always ready for a challenge, spoke up. He laughed and said, "And which do you seek to do? Build or fish? As for my brother and me, we are only fishermen."

Jesus let the perfectly repaired net drop. He looked at us, from one to the other. And though his eyes shone with happiness, this time there was no smile. James and I were too astonished to move when Jesus grasped our hands, one in each of his and pulled us powerfully, easily to our feet. *Follow Me, and I will make you fish for people.* [Matthew 4:19]

I remember to this moment the feel of Jesus' hand on mine. His grip was powerful, much more compelling than what I would have imagined from his appearance. But it was not the grasp of some man trying to outdo or vanquish another man. He was not attempting to establish strength or superiority, though God alone knows how vastly stronger and superior

Jesus was to us, both younger men and foolishly full of our own notions of strength and vitality. But the power that flowed through those roughened hands was not that of mere strength, but rather that of authority. From the moment Jesus grasped my hand and James' hand, he was in command of our lives. He became the author of our stories from that day forward. There was both a gentleness and a capability that could be felt in that moment, and we trusted him enough to get up and leave everything behind. As we joined Simon and Andrew and walked away, I barely heard Zebedee calling angrily after us. All of that and more was communicated in one clasp of those hands.

And, oh, what I have seen these poor, ruined hands do in the past three years! Yes, of course, there have been the great and renowned miracles—the ones that everyone knows about, the ones that James predicted would bring us to this dark day. I saw these hands twice lift a few loaves and fishes heavenward, only to have over 9,000 men fed along with their families. I was there when these hands beckoned Lazarus to rise and leave the tomb he'd been in for four days. I accompanied Jesus into the child's room when he raised her from death with these hands, instructing her mesmerized and overjoyed parents to give her something to eat. I witnessed these hands write never-to-be-admitted names in the dirt while the mob cried out for the blood of an adulterous woman. I watched these hands raise lepers who were bowed to the ground, only to see their rotted flesh healed and glowing with vitality. Before my very eyes, these hands mixed dirt with spittle to make mud that gave a blind man sight.

These are just a few of the miracles worked by these hands that are known to the world. But I saw those miracles and kindnesses that the world did not witness and would not have counted for much if they had. I was with Peter and his wife and family when Jesus placed these hands upon their mother to banish her fever. And I smiled to see how swiftly she rose to her feet to bring us all water to wash, and food and wine to eat. I watched these hands lift the unclean cup given by the unclean Samaritan woman to his lips and drink the water no other Jew would touch. And I saw the woman who offered it redeemed and purified by this simple gesture and all it signified, so that she could become a messenger of salvation to her own people. I saw hundreds, thousands, of women and children touched or comforted or held by these hands, only to go away changed and rejoicing, without even knowing why. I was among those whom Jesus rebuked for driving away children who craved only his touch.

I observed these hands as they washed garments dirtied by long trips on dusty roads, made cooking fires, roasted fish, carved small and exquisite figures for gifts, waved with laughter, gestured while teaching, washed feet, broke bread, drank wine, clasped others in dance, kneaded sore and tense muscles, gripped a staff for the journey, embraced his mother, lifted Simon's gleeful children to swing them through the air, replenished charcoal fires on cold mornings, pulled cloaks close over sleeping disciples against the chill of the desert night, sowed seed with farmers, fished with fishermen, herded sheep with shepherds, picked grapes with wine-makers and olives with olive-growers and figs with orchard workers, built dwellings with carpenters, lifted up the holy Scripture with rabbis, wiped away tears, pointed at Pharisees, lifted burdens from those too old or tired to carry them. In even the smallest gesture of these hands, I beheld the prospect of renewal and redemption.

*Everyone around me is silent now,* listening to the sound of my wrenching sobs. The centurion bent down and took the nails away. I felt Salome's presence close behind me, but she did not touch me. My other mother, his mother, Mary, is a little apart from us, bent to the ground in her own unfathomable mourning. My tears fall upon his holy hands, mixing with the water I poured over them to cleanse them as best I could. I hold them in my own tight grasp, thinking, foolishly, to warm them. I can't accept these hands stilled forever. I don't know who can do their work. No one. But I know that if the past three years are to mean anything at all, if my life is to mean anything at all, I will have to try. After all, was I not one of the first works of these precious hands?

# REFLECTING *on the* STORY

We know from the gospels that Jesus worked many miracles with his hands. But can we even begin to imagine everything accomplished by those hands? Can we guess at the magnitude, not just of the unrecorded miracles, but of the daily tasks, the gentle touches, the encouraging pats on the back, the brief clasps, the passing gestures, the helping? John's gospel itself ends with the testimony that *there are also many other things that Jesus did; if every one of them were written down, I suppose that the world itself could not contain the books that would be written.* (John 21:25)

Are we not in the same position as John in that we, too, are the works of Jesus' hands? Jesus is One with the creator God who formed us and with the creative Spirit who gives us life and guidance. Because we are, indeed, among the works of Jesus' hands, we have the opportunity to use our own hands and bodies and spirits to do God's work in the world today. We have a tremendous advantage over John who mourned at the foot of the cross in that we know "the rest of the story," as the radio personality Paul Harvey used to say. We have already been baptized and received the Holy Spirit, and we are no longer paralyzed by the tragedy of Good Friday.

Yet even in the midst of his anguish, John was ready to follow Jesus' instructions. We know from Scripture that John took Mary into his home and cared for her from that moment on. John was the only one of the male apostles who had the courage to boldly follow Jesus into the courtyard of the high priest and then, a few long hours later, to Calvary. And it was John who believed Mary Magdalene's words about Jesus rising, so much so that he outran even Peter as they hurried to the grave. Before John *knew*...he believed, and he acted.

John was not the beloved apostle simply because he was a young man who followed Jesus around like a puppy. John was beloved because he used the love Jesus had and taught to change himself and the world around him. John was a physical person; he worked with his body and his hands. In fact, Jesus—and the rest of us—first meet John at work mending fishing nets. From the gospel descriptions, we envision John constantly in motion: fishing, mending nets, flinging aside everything to follow Jesus, climbing the mountain to see Jesus transfigured in conversation with Moses and Elijah, supporting Mary at the foot of the cross, racing to the tomb, following Peter and the risen Jesus on the beach, and later, as tradition tells us, living longer than any other apostle and traveling the known world to preach the Gospel.

John is not someone who talks about work and action; he's someone who acts. In this, he followed Jesus, just as we can follow John's example. How can we act as Jesus' hands in our daily lives? Simply. We need not demonstrate profundity or piety. We can show those we encounter that we belong to Jesus through a gesture or a kind word. Jesus mended lives; John mended nets; we can mend hurt feelings. We can reach out to someone at work or in our community who has been dismissed by others or has felt the sting of discrimination. A gentle word can change a person's day, if not their life. An accompanying hand outstretched in friendship or greeting might be the only human touch some people will experience on any given day—or week, or month, or year.

Jesus walked the length and breadth of Israel, John walked with him, and we can walk a block or two with a neighbor who seems lonely, a co-worker who needs to exercise at lunch time, a friend who is stressed, a spouse who is having a hard time expressing feelings. We can use our hands to support an elderly person stepping off a curb, taking out the garbage, or crossing the street. We can carry a child who is tired or cranky, pick up a grocery bag, haul a bag of laundry.

Jesus arranged for the care of his mother; John took on her care, and we can care for someone who is bereft or in mourning. Remember here that John did not just comfort Mary through Jesus' death: *and from that hour the disciple took her into his own home* (John 19:27). Often we dutifully attend wakes and funerals, and then move on with our lives just when the person who is most deeply experiencing the loss feels most profoundly alone. That's when we can carry over a casserole, extend a hand in invitation, open a car door to take the bereaved to an appointment, lunch, or just for a ride. We can sit and simply hold the person's hand in prayer and in silence.

Jesus hurried to the house of Jairus to raise his daughter despite the mocking of the crowds; John raced to the empty tomb despite the doubt of others; we can rush to raise the spirits of those around us who feel downcast or hopeless despite the fact that we are busy or don't really believe we can be much help. Mother Teresa famously told those who felt inadequate in the face of her goodness that every effort to love or help another counts in the eyes of God. We can listen to a friend who is downhearted. We can steer someone who is unemployed and discouraged to an agency or training program. We can help someone who needs therapy figure out how to afford it or how to seek community services. We can drive or arrange for transportation for someone who needs to join a support or church-based counseling group. We can accompany someone to church.

Finally, after Jesus' ascension and the gift of the Holy Spirit on Pentecost, John was believed to have traveled far and wide to spread the Good News. Imagine how extraordinary that must have been. Here was John, who'd hardly left the unsophisticated environs of Galilee for most of his youth and young adulthood, first giving up everything he'd known to follow Jesus, and then, giving up even his native country to preach Jesus. Galilee could not even boast the diversity and urbanity of Jerusalem, visited by Jews from all over the world and traders from every nation. Although Galilee was probably a step up from Jesus' supposed hometown, Nazareth, they were both what we might call today "out in the sticks" when compared to the religious and trading cities of that time. And yet, John, despite his lack of experience and the narrow focus of his life, plunged into the greater world. Was he fearless? Probably not. He was an apostle, not a superhero. But the call of Jesus, and then the Spirit of God, powered him through any uncertainty and fear he might have felt.

John literally pushed through every boundary of his life, eventually breaking through any limit that would keep him from Jesus and Jesus' work. This is what we, too, are called to do in our effort to manifest Jesus in our world, and it is probably the hardest part of discipleship. To leave our comfort zones, to push past our cherished and well-built boundaries, to explore the very limits of our physical and spiritual boundaries—this is a monumental challenge for most of us. And most of us will need to take on this challenge little by little. John did not go from mending fish nets one minute, to watching Jesus die on the cross the next, to preaching the resurrection in foreign lands the next. It was a long physical and spiritual journey that he took, with Jesus, one step at a time. So can we.

## PRAYER

*Saint John, beloved friend and apostle of Jesus, you were the one who was probably closest to the Lord during his ministry. You experienced Jesus in ways we cannot even imagine. He taught you how to use your body, mind, and spirit in his service. Teach me how to use my hands and feet, my ears and voice, my intelligence and skills, and my possessions and gifts to reveal Jesus to everyone I encounter, especially those in need. John, you knew Jesus physically in life, death, and resurrection; I can only know him spiritually, so help me to use my own body to express that knowledge. Give me the courage to follow your example beyond what is familiar and safe to me. Help me to race, in hope and joy, to the empty tomb; and when I have fully experienced its glory, help me to show it to others. Amen.*

## PRAYERFULLY ASK YOURSELF

1. When is the last time I consciously reached out to take someone's hand in greeting or touched another's arm or shoulder with gentle encouragement? How have others reacted when I have—and when I have not—reached out in healing ways?

2. When I am in church, how do those around me respond when I do—and when I don't—reach my hands out to greet them?

3. When have we felt what John may have felt at hearing Jesus' words? How did we come to understand that Jesus does not always give us precisely what we think we need?

## TAKE ACTION

Do something today to stretch your personal, physical boundaries in the service of Jesus or in an effort to show Jesus to others. Challenge yourself; in other words, if you love hugging people, giving someone a hug doesn't qualify as stretching your boundaries! However, if you are not comfortable showing physical affection, warmly shake someone's hand; surprise your child with an after-school hug; hook arms with your spouse or a friend. Go to a church in another community to experience the diversity of the faithful. Exercise your body by walking, jogging, or biking while saying a prayer for someone you dislike or are uncomfortable with. Pick up trash on a playground or at a park. Offer to grocery shop for an elderly or shut-in neighbor. Thank God for the ability to use your body to move outside your comfort zone in his service.

# Three

# MARY MAGDALENE

*She stood behind him, at his feet, weeping, and began to bathe his feet with her tears and to dry them with her hair. Then she continued kissing his feet and anointing them with the ointment. Then turning toward the woman, he said, "I* **tell you, her sins, which were many, have been forgiven; hence she has shown great love."** Luke 7:38, 44, 47

I AM NOT AFRAID OF DISTURBING MARY IN HER EXTREME GRIEF, for I can see she has no awareness of anyone or anything besides the body of her son that lies clasped close in her arms. She is insensible to everything else, all that is happening around us. The continuing rain from the violent storm released by the heavens when he died has become a cloak of cold, heavy mist. It falls lightly but hangs heavily upon us as though the saints and the angels and even God cannot keep from weeping. My robes are heavy with it; they weigh me down as I move

45

uselessly about, trying to be of help, trying to do what I can.

Trying not to think. Trying not to remember.

I watch John, who has just helped take Jesus down from the cross, and there is a change in him. After he finally brought himself to wrench out the nails, something shifted in John. His grief has strengthened into a determination that I cannot fully comprehend. It is as though this smothering haze of rain has hardened into ice around him, and he seems in my eyes to flash and glimmer with this newness, like morning frost in the dawning sun. The transformation in this naive young man who was so devoted to Jesus confuses and frightens me a little. Where did this courage come from? How did those soft, dark eyes become so full of fire?

As to the others here, well, to be honest, I hardly know them. I've traveled on the edge of this group while trying to make Jesus the center of my life. It has not been easy. I know that some of the other followers despise me and would wish me away were it not for Jesus' love and forgiveness of me. Now they will, undoubtedly, have their way. Now I will be rejected again, for my chance to continue in the new life, to be welcomed, has surely died with Jesus. I will become again the outsider, the sinner, the one marked with shame and illness.

No one here at this moment, in the bleak, muddy aftermath of this unspeakable death, will drive me away, but I am not foolish enough to think they will defend me or strive to keep me among them. John is a good boy, but he is charged now with Mary, and all his thoughts and efforts will be for her. Who knows what danger she, as Jesus' mother, is in from the Roman occupiers and the enraged Pharisees? John has his life's work before him in this sorrow-stricken woman holding her son.

Yes, Mary might help me, might shield me, but look at her!

Will she ever recover from what she has seen this past day? These last few hours, especially, would be enough to destroy the mind and soul of any mother, never mind one who must have had such high hopes, such strong dreams, for her blessed son. And even if she were conscious of my sadness, my loss, my plight, I don't think I could ask for her support. I have never felt comfortable with her, not because she hasn't been kind to me; she has been the kindest woman I've known. Just the passing touch of her hand, gentle as the fluttering of a dove's wings, upon my oft-furrowed brow these past months and years has soothed me. Still, she never seeks to talk or asks me any questions or seeks me out. I feel deep within myself that she is too far above and beyond me to be easily ap-proached. *She is his mother!* It is enough just to know that she hasn't driven me from serving him; I would never ask Mary for another thing.

The others I know even less, though it is certain that Salome does not love me. She has grown indifferent to me in these latter days, but at first, she looked upon me with such derision and dismay that I could never bring myself to meet her heated stare. I'm sure that she chided Jesus on more than one occa-sion for letting me join the disciples, for Salome holds back nothing! To have seen her and Mary in the same place with Jesus, you would have guessed that Salome was the mother the way she spoke boldly, trying to tell him what to do and worry-ing over him endlessly. When she could be with us, she alone would supervise the washing of his clothes and preparation of his food, insisting that the younger disciples were "no good at anything that required a bit of sense." During such times, when Salome would harangue Jesus until he teased her or grew tired and went off alone to pray, I would see a small and indulgent, but knowing, smile come upon Mary's face. At the moment that smile dawned, if you were paying attention, you would know who was the real mother.

Salome failed to turn Jesus, or her sons John and James, for that matter, against me, but to her credit, she did not maintain her hostility toward me for very long. It is not in her lively nature to hold a grudge, and while she never welcomed me or seemed pleased when I came around, she did grow accustomed to my presence and stopped making such sour faces when Jesus—never mind John or James!—spoke to me. I cannot blame her for the distance she keeps from me. No one is comfortable around disease, and I have carried the marks of disease for much of my life. I secretly fear that even after Jesus healed me, the signs can still be seen in me.

It is natural for people to fear and reject those who are ill; human nature does not want any reminders of physical and emotional frailty. People do not want to see someone who is broken, for it reminds them of how easily they might break. The healthy turn away from the sick, even if they've witnessed the healing of the one who'd been ill. So it is with Salome. I think at heart she is a good woman, but I have been hurt by many a "good" man and woman in my day, and I will not count on Salome to take my part or insist that I stay with the disciples.

Will there even *be* disciples now? Will there be a group for me to follow, to find comfort in, even if they would accept me? What will become of Jesus' followers? Apart from the threat to us all now, around whom would we gather? Who would be our teacher, leader, Lord? Is it possible that we will, in our fear and ruinous disappointment, now scatter to the four winds, more lost than before Jesus found us?

All these around me are suffering, but none of them suffers

in quite the same manner as I. Each of them has lost the center of their lives in losing Jesus: Mary has lost a son; John, a friend and teacher; Salome, a master; Joseph and Nicodemus, a colleague and rabbi. And the poor centurion? Well, he is wandering around as if he has lost his mind.

But I, I have lost all of this and more. Jesus was all of these things to me, my only friend, master, teacher, rabbi—and all I will ever have in the way of brother, father, husband, though by human standards he was none of these. But to me, Jesus was everything and more. He was my physician and healer. No one here in this dark garden can say that. Yes, certainly, he healed all in one way or another. But me! He healed me, body, mind, and spirit. No one who has not experienced this can fully understand. I barely understand it myself, but oh! I remember what it felt like! I knew what it was to be shackled by illness and sin for as long as I could remember, only to have all that lifted in a moment, at a word. An impossible thing, and yes, Jesus did it!

And now? What happens now? For in addition to the sorrow I share with these people, there is my shameful, selfish secret. I am paralyzed by fear, and not the fear the rest of the apostles and disciples have of the Romans or the Sanhedrin. Not only do I mourn the loss of the one who was everything to me, I cannot stop myself from wondering…will I lose the miracle of health that he bestowed upon me? Now that Jesus is gone, will these gifts go as well? Even as my heart breaks with grief, I am acutely conscious of my body and mind. I search myself for indications of the disease returning. I know every symptom, from the mildest trembling, to the smallest fever, to the contorting anguish that can grasp me and shake me like a sycamore leaf in a wind storm. I am helpless against it without my Lord. What do I do if it comes back to crush me in its grip? How much more devastating it will be now to fall under the power of sickness when I have known health! Where is Jesus today, who is my only hope and help?

I look up and see that Mary still cradles the body, her eyes unseeing of all but what is inside her mind and memories. Slowly, driven to my knees by fear and desperation, I creep toward them, my robe dragging in the mud. I can no longer claim sanity or wit, only the pressing need to be near Jesus. I find myself by these poor cut and calloused feet, punctured by the nail. I reach out, weeping, and embrace them, lowering my face until it rests upon the cold flesh and my tears mingle with the rain, slowly rinsing away the blood and filth. I want to die. Here. And now.

*Suddenly my closed eyes are filled with another day.* I am surrounded by color and warmth and music and aromas so tantalizing they make me hungry. The room is rich, hung with tapestries, and the low table is covered with food fit for a banquet. And so it is: a banquet given in Jesus' honor, but that is just the surface of it. There is more to it than festivity. The Pharisees who have invited Jesus do not intend in their hearts to honor, but rather to test and, if possible, find an error that they might declare and condemn before the people. Even in those early days, they feared what Jesus' authority and popularity might mean for them. Some around this laden table are merely curious, a few even friendly, but the most powerful here tonight do not wish Jesus well.

I should not even be here. Jesus has just recently healed me, and I am out of my mind with the joy of health and gratitude. And, of course, I love him. What woman does not love the physician who cures her? I would stay near Jesus always if it were allowed, for even in these first days of health, I nurse this secret fear that in his absence, I will fall prey again to disease. But still, I know I should not have come to this house. There are religious men, important men, at this feast, and they know me for a sinner. They know I have been ill most of my life, and they do not believe me truly well, despite what they have heard about Jesus performing this miracle. I see it in their twisted expressions, their hateful eyes like coals burning in their heads, their sneering lips, their hurried efforts to pull their robes and their food far away from me so I will not contaminate them. I see the most powerful among them glance from me to Jesus and back; they watch avidly, with a greed that wakens me to their intent.

I realize with a sinking heart that I have made a terrible mistake! In my zeal to be near Jesus, to be of service, I have put my Lord in a terrible position. He came here to teach and socialize, perhaps to convince a few of these pious men to become disciples. He accepted this invitation in the hope, I am sure, of converting enemies into friends. But how can Jesus do that now, with me in their midst, like a lost dog skulking after its owner? I am something to be ashamed of, to be kept hidden away, for the dark and silent moments of the night. They will surely use me against my Lord.

I have crouched behind where Jesus reclines at the table, at his feet, but now I stopper the perfumed ointment I have bought with half my savings, and start to creep back out of the room. At that moment, Jesus turns and looks at me. I don't think I can bear to meet his steady gaze and see the embarrassment and chastisement that must certainly be there, and yet my eyes are drawn upwards slowly until I am looking into his. My heart ceases for several beats and then begins to pulse wildly, for what I see in Jesus' eyes is not condemnation, but acceptance and, yes, even approval! He wants me to be here! He knows how much damage my presence and what I have come for might do to his reputation, and still he is glad to see me. How can this be? What is Jesus thinking? Then, abruptly, it doesn't matter. I don't need to know why or understand the meaning of this love, only that it is there for me.

My eyes fill before I even taste the tears in my throat, and I began to weep silent, copious tears. It seems to me that the cleansing stream that Jesus sent through my body can no longer be contained within it and is pouring out of me. I bend my head over the travel-worn feet that I have come to love, and drops from the stream within me fall upon them. His feet are worn and dirty; I notice that the Pharisee has given no water for Jesus to wash. I see the path of my tears form tiny rivers in the sand and dust on his feet, tracing the blue veins that stand out in taut relief against the skin.

No longer thinking or registering the alarmed murmurs of the other men in the room, I swiftly remove the old sandals as my tears continue to fall. His feet are now wet with what I have held inside me for a lifetime, and the dirt that is dried upon them begins to loosen. I quickly remove the hood of my robe and, ignoring the gasps of horror, begin to rub Jesus' feet clean and dry with my long, thick hair. When I finish and my hair is damp with my own tears and dull with the dirt from his feet, I pull the stopper from the jar of ointment. As soon as the scent rises, I know the men around this table understand how expensive this perfume is, for these are men who are accustomed to fine things. I know they are calculating the cost of it and how I came to purchase it, to afford it. If I were sensible to anything but Jesus, I would be hurt and angered by their assumptions, but I no longer care. I have come here for this, and I will accomplish my purpose.

I am beside myself with love and gratitude. I begin to kiss Jesus' feet. The room is in an all-but-silent uproar. I hear their furious buzzing as I would a swarm of locusts, and they mean no more to me than that. They are waiting for Jesus to react, to stop me, probably to kick out and send me sprawling. But Jesus has not said one word or moved a muscle other than to let me lift his feet. When I finish kissing them, I pour the ointment upon them. All of it. In this, if in little else in my life until now, I am extravagantly generous. I use every drop, and it flows over his feet and makes a pool, thickly soaking into the floor beneath. The aroma is overwhelming, covering even the various cooking odors from the untouched food on the table. It will be a great while before the fragrance leaves this house; these Pharisees will long remember me.

Finally, I lift my eyes to Jesus' face. His eyes are filled with tears of understanding and even joy. He smiles at me as though I am the only person in this room. Softly, Jesus lays a hand upon my head. I know I have done his reputation great harm, and I know that he knows this, too; but it doesn't seem to matter.

"What degradation!" I hear one of them mutter, and I almost laugh aloud. Degradation? I have known degradation, and this is no such thing. Degradation is spending your life in the corner, the shadow, the twilight. Degradation is keeping your gaze cast down for fear of what you will see in the eyes of others. Degradation is knowing that everything about you signals dis-ease, contamination, sin. Degradation is rejection.

But this? This is glorious! This is forgiveness, another form of healing from Jesus. This is comprehension, affirmation of my humanity, knowledge that I am loved and accepted by the only one in this place, in the world I know, who matters. With this, I can go out into that world in the firm understanding that I have been transformed by love.

### I come back to myself kneeling in the mud of Calvary, my face chilled by the damp and the cold flesh of my Lord's feet. I see a small jar that has been set beside me and look up to see Salome walking away. Nicodemus, I know, has brought aloes and oil for anointing the dead, and Salome has somehow overcome her indifference to me enough to offer me this small gift. I lift the oil and pour it over his feet, rubbing it in vigorously as if I can warm back to life that which is dead. But no man or woman can do that. As my hands work in the oil, I realize that there is really only one thing I can do. I can take the gifts that Jesus has given me—of healing, forgiveness, acceptance—and share them with others, regardless of my own fears. That, after all, is just what he asked of all of us. Until now, I had not thought myself worthy enough to act upon that instruction. Who, I mocked myself, would listen to you?

But here I am, a witness to the agonizing sacrifice, again prostrate at Jesus' feet. It doesn't matter who will listen to me; it matters that I have listened to him. It doesn't matter that I am afraid; surely he was afraid when they pounded the nails into the feet I cradle in my hands. It doesn't matter that I am weak; the weakness of this crucifixion has revealed the meaning of strength. I will use my own feet to follow in his footsteps.

## REFLECTING ON THE STORY

Apocryphal stories and gospels suggest that Mary Magdalene did, indeed, travel extensively to spread the word of Jesus. It may be that she accompanied John and Mary to Ephesus. A woman who had been rejected and despised by just about everyone who met her became one of the most devout and productive disciples who ever lived. There are churches and religious institutions named after her in just about every corner of the world where Christianity is known. Her "footprints" are indeed widely dispersed.

Why does Mary Magdalene strike such a chord with believers all over the world, despite being so little known in terms of her actual story? Of all those who followed Jesus all the way to Calvary, Mary Magdalene is the one about whom very few facts are established, and yet, she is perhaps most like us. She is very human in all the ways we may wish *not* to be human. She is frightened, she has been disastrously ill, she is a sinner, and she has been rejected and scorned. She is, most of all, vulnerable to relapsing into any of these states. At least she feels herself to be, and she must struggle hard to hold onto what Jesus has given her.

Do we not sometimes find ourselves feeling like Mary probably felt? Most of us worry about what others think of us. We wonder whether we are accepted by the "right" people, the people we most want to impress, the people with power and authority. We worry about falling ill—physically, mentally, or spiritually; and if we have already been seriously ill, the way Mary Magdalene was ill, we worry about relapsing into our former state. We wonder, to our secret shame: if God has cured us once, will he cure us again? How many cancer survivors feel completely free of the disease, or of worrying about its potential return? How many people with addictions don't worry about falling again into that dark hole? How many survivors of heart attack or cardiovascular disease don't feel anxious when their pulses race or they are short of breath?

Also like Mary Magdalene, we too have experienced sin and, hopefully, have sought and received God's forgiveness. But do we feel fully forgiven? Do we wonder whether sin will overtake us again? Is there a part of us that wonders whether God really *did* forgive us, or will continue to do so? It is easy to identify with the idea of Mary wondering whether she can remain healthy and forgiven and sane if Jesus is not beside her providing constant encouragement. It is part of our human nature to fear falling back into vulnerable states of illness and sin even when we know and believe that Jesus has healed and forgiven us.

However, we also know what Mary Magdalene was just learning: that Jesus is never absent to us as long as we seek him. We need not worry about "losing" the Lord's encouragement, healing, forgiveness, and grace, because as long as we want these things from Jesus, he provides them. He does not leave us; only we can leave him.

Following Mary's example, we can use our feet to walk beside Jesus *and* to walk in his way, for they are, really, one and the same. If we keep ourselves in Jesus' presence, we cannot help but do the work he does. Unlike Mary, we need not travel far to manifest Jesus in our world. We can walk to church or a parish meeting. We can walk through a park or street, deliberately greeting everyone we pass. We can invite a friend or acquaintance who is suffering grief or trouble to take a sunset stroll with us. We can enter a walk-a-thon to benefit a good cause. We can walk regularly for exercise and communication with a spouse or family members. We can pass up a prime parking spot in order to leave it for someone who may need it more, even if it means walking a longer distance to our destination. We can walk into a convalescent home or hospital to visit someone who needs company. We can walk away from an argument or conflict. We can donate new or nearly comfortable shoes and new socks to the Salvation Army, Goodwill, or other organizations that help clothe the poor.

There are unlimited ways we can use our feet *for* Jesus and to keep close *to* Jesus. With every step, we leave fear and disease behind as we walk more firmly in the confidence of Jesus' love and constant presence.

### PRAYER

*Saint Mary Magdalene, two thousand years from the time you walked the earth, you still have an uncertain reputation. People still differ on who and what you were. But no one can equivocate upon who you became: one of Jesus' most faithful and diligent disciples, willing to risk your life to serve him and others. Grant me the courage to accept Jesus' healing and forgiveness and to follow him with my whole heart and mind and body. Let me learn from you how to make deep and lasting sacrifices so that everyone who meets me will know I serve Christ. Help me to lay my illnesses and my sins down at the foot of the cross, and then, to leave them there as I join you in rejoicing in the Lord's resurrection. Help me to allow my weaknesses to reveal God's strength. Teach me how to develop confidence in Christ so that I worry less about my reputation and more about my vocation. Strengthen me so that I refuse to let any person or thing or opinion keep me from God. Show me how to go confidently wherever my feet lead me in following the risen Jesus. Amen.*

## PRAYERFULLY ASK YOURSELF

1. How do I serve Jesus in whatever places my feet take me each day?

2. When was the last time I surrendered in an effort to follow Jesus in word and deed because I told myself I was not strong enough or worthy enough?

3. In what ways have we felt, like Mary Magdalene, that Jesus may have abandoned us? How have we welcomed Jesus back into our lives in those times?

## TAKE ACTION

Is there anything in your life that holds you back from fully following Jesus? Consider whether there is a sin or failing or particular incident that you have not addressed but that may be limiting you. It may be something relatively small—like snapping at an elderly relative or neighbor—that you've half-dismissed, telling yourself, "it's just not that important." It could be something so monumental—like seriously harming another person—that you've buried it deep because you can't bring yourself to deal with it or even acknowledge it. Perhaps it is something in between—like a nasty exchange between you and your spouse or best friend—that it has been festering for some time and seems to become more oppressive and weighty as time goes by. These are the kinds of things that can become, like Mary Magdalene's fears and illnesses, obstacles between us and God. Without us fully realizing it, these burdens can keep us from becoming complete and confident followers of Jesus. Today, select an issue that may be limiting your participation in the body of Christ, and address it. Openly and honestly confess this thing to God, and ask for forgiveness. Resolve to try to avoid such a sin in the future. Most importantly, accept God's forgiveness and healing, for in cases like this, they are one and the same. Finally, if there is another person involved in this issue, ask them for forgiveness, and make whatever physical, emotional, or spiritual restitution you can. If you cannot deal directly with the individual, take a different step, like offering in that individual's name/memory a special kindness to another person, or making a gift of money or your time to an organization favored by the individual you've wronged. When you have done everything you can to address this obstacle to following Jesus, let it go and move forward in God's love and forgiveness.

## Four

# NICODEMUS

*Now there was a Pharisee named Nicodemus, a leader of the Jews. He came to Jesus by night and said...'Rabbi, we know that you are a teacher who has come from God; for no one can do these signs...apart from the presence of God.' Jesus answered him, "Very truly, I tell you, no one can see the kingdom of God without being born from above."*

**JOHN 3:1-3**

**MY SERVANTS ARE AGHAST THAT I INSIST ON CARRYING THIS MIXTURE OF MYRRH AND ALOES BY MYSELF.** They cry that it is too heavy, that I am an old man, that it is beneath my dignity to be seen dragging such a burden through the streets. My dignity! What is my dignity to me now? How can I care for my reputation, my role as a Pharisee, my title as a teacher of Israel?

I worried too much about all of those things, and my fear blinded me to what was right there before me. Jesus the Christ! The answer that I and my people have been waiting for through the ages, and I didn't let myself see it, wouldn't allow my stubborn dignity to acknowledge what my mind and heart were telling me. Where was my dignity when I was skulking about in the dark, circling the periphery of Jesus' followers, waiting for a moment when I might slip to his side unnoticed? Where was my dignity when I refused to meet the curious glances of other disciples because I feared they would know and expose me? Where was my dignity when I worried that someone important, one of my brethren, might see me associating with those they considered enemies?

I would drag this weight of myrrh and aloes across the world if I thought it could restore what has been lost by my dignity! For it was upon my dignity that I stood last night when the leaders of the Sanhedrin had gathered and were prepared to condemn Jesus. Did I insist that this should not be done? Did I demand they convene the full council from all over the country before making such a condemnation? Did I put myself between Jesus and those who beat and mocked him? Did I confront Caiphas and Annas directly and declare, in front of all assembled, that their plan was evil and self-serving?

No, no. My dignity—my fear—wouldn't allow me to take such rash steps. Oh, I spoke up for Jesus, certainly, warned them against collaborating with the Romans in the killing of one of our own. I tried to appeal to their sense of national righteousness. I counseled them against being seen as belonging to Rome, the despised occupier. But my arguments were not strong enough, not loud enough, not violent enough. I had learned my lesson, hadn't I, at the Feast of Booths when I first defended Jesus publicly? My brother Pharisees and the chief priests had sent the temple guards to arrest Jesus for disturbing the peace of the people at the festival, but the guards had returned empty-handed, themselves stunned by Jesus' teaching and presence. I'd thought this to be my opportunity to advance the case for Jesus or, at least, to show my brothers that they were wrong to harass him. After all, I reasoned, if our guard, the most brutal and unfeeling among us, could be moved by Jesus, why not those of us who bore the knowledge of the nation upon our shoulders?

But I'd miscalculated the violence of feeling some of the Pharisees had against Jesus. Even then, my words were weak, posed as a question to bring the brethren back to their senses rather than the declaration of Jesus' righteousness that it should have been. *"Our law does not judge people without first giving them a hearing to find out what they are doing, does it?"* [John 7:51] I cringe now to think of my frail effort, my cowardly inquiry. Yet, even then, with such a puny challenge, they turned upon me instantly. *"Surely you are not also from Galilee, are you? Search and you will see that no prophet is to arise from Galilee."* [John 7:52]

Such was their fear and hatred of Jesus that they would scorn and deride a fellow Pharisee who had been at council with them for years. But at that moment, I thought only for myself, *my dignity!* That my brothers would treat me that way affected me deeply. Certainly we had been at odds before, all of us, on any number of issues. How to deal with the Roman occupation? How to keep the people faithful in the face of so much adversity and idolatry? How to feed those who couldn't continue to work under the Roman boot? And of course we spent hours, days, much of our lives debating the holy Scripture with one another. What exactly did God expect from us with this commandment? What did Moses mean by this law? How did this phrase impact the one before it and the whole teaching? About such things we could argue forever, and did.

But there was always an underlying respect for every learned brother who came to the table with something to offer. As lively as the discussions could become, no one ever left in anger or hurt, because all were heard and every idea duly pondered.

So when the other Pharisees and chief priests attacked me so harshly for simply asking a question—and we all knew the proper answer, though none articulated it that day—I retreated. Instead of comprehending how strong a stand some among us had already taken against Jesus, I stumbled back. I was afraid for my dignity, the position of respect I held among them. I even told myself that if I really wanted to help Jesus, I should keep myself in good standing among them for future challenges. I should keep my mouth closed. I clung to that pathetic rationalization just like I clung to my dignity, and by the time the Sanhedrin met last night to condemn Jesus, I was too afraid to do anything more than plead feebly for him.

What was I thinking? So many things, all in conflict. I did truly believe that Pontius Pilate might put a stop to this disaster. Pilate was having enough trouble governing for Caesar; the last thing he needed was the crucifixion of this well-known preacher. Pilate, I told myself, would have the common sense to stop this. Or even Herod, for I had heard how the superstitious fool feared that Jesus was his punishment for having beheaded John the Baptist. An appeal to Herod, who would never be free from his own fears, would save Jesus. The Sanhedrin would not succeed, I told myself; if the law did not allow us to put one of our own people to death, then the high priest and his father-in-law certainly wouldn't be able to convince other authorities to do this despicable thing for them.

I never imagined that my brothers had been clever and deceitful enough to thwart Pilate's intention by filling the courtyard with rioters crying for Jesus to die. When I saw paid ruffians screaming for Barabbas rather than Jesus, I finally came to understand just how determined the leaders of the Sanhedrin were. And then, Herod. How could I forget that the man is half-insane with guilt and debauchery? His diseased mind could not bear to have one as pure and truth-filled as Jesus in his palace, never mind the world.

None of the events or people I'd told myself would intervene to save Jesus did. How could this have happened? We let it happen. I let it happen.

But, I wasn't sure! I didn't know! We'd been taught from Scripture to expect the Messiah to be so powerful and filled with charisma that it would be impossible to wonder, to question whether this was the one. It would have been clear, blindingly obvious. There would have been lights and angels and trumpets, and the world would have paid obeisance. Where were the trappings of royalty and magnificence? Where was the indomitable voice and righteous judgment in Jesus, impoverished, wearing old clothes and eating whatever was set before him?

With Jesus, nothing was simple. How many ways did we ask him to declare himself the Messiah, only to have him speak in riddles! It was as if he enjoyed confounding us! Even at the Festival of Booths where I tried to defend Jesus, his behavior made it so difficult to provide any protection! Seeing and hearing him throughout the temple, agitating the people and enraging the Pharisees with words that were impossible to hear or understand, made me wonder. It chilled me to hear him accuse us, *"Did not Moses give you the law? Yet none of you keeps the law. Why are you looking for an opportunity to kill me?"* [John 7:19] When my brethren suggested that Jesus might start a riot, I feared that they were right. He had the crowds in an absolute tumult. I let my dignity, my fear, whisper in my ear, "Would the Messiah do this?"

And so, God forgive me, I again allowed myself to doubt when my brothers flung at me their denial that a prophet could come from Galilee. This is true, I told myself in the face of their derision. The Scriptures do not speak of a prophet, and certainly not the Messiah, born in Galilee. I kept that question, the instant when I betrayed Jesus, deep inside me as a tiny spark of hope that maybe Jesus wasn't the one; maybe I hadn't abandoned the Savior of Israel. So it was that I came to weep publicly for the first time early this morning, when, standing beside his mother when Pilate condemned him, she said softly, as though to herself, "We are so far from Bethlehem."

Knowing that her mind must have been confused by the horror of what we were witnessing, I said gently, "Not so far, Mary, just a few hours walk south of here."

She smiled through her pain at the poor fool that I am. "I know of Bethlehem. My son was born there."

*She is losing her reason*, I thought sadly, but she shook her head gently at my pitying glance and continued, "It was the time of the great census, and my husband was forced to return to Bethlehem where he was born, to register. Jesus was born the night we arrived. Caesar was doing God's work with that census, making us fulfill the words of the prophet: *'And you, Bethlehem, in the land of Judah, are by no means least among the rulers of Judah; for from you shall come a Ruler who is to shepherd my people Israel.'*" [Matthew 2:6]

Mary's words struck me like one hundred blows. Jesus was born not in Nazareth of Galilee where he lived as a boy, but in Bethlehem, the city of the Messiah. I'd fallen to my knees this morning beside Mary, and, in the midst of her great suffering, she bent and clasped my shoulders in her strong hands. She heard me muttering, "It cannot be true. It cannot." Misinterpreting my devastation, she assured me, "Yes, Nicodemus, oh yes! God was determined that Jesus experience all that the prophet said of the Messiah. For we were forced to flee Herod, and God led us into Egypt when Jesus was young. And so, God fulfilled another of the prophecies: *'Out of Egypt I have called My son.'*" [Matthew 2:15]

She continued speaking to me softly, thinking to comfort me and not knowing that every word fell upon me like the lash of a whip. She told of the great light in the night sky at the time of the birth; how the wise and learned men from all over the world came and paid her infant son obeisance, leaving untold wealth; how angels descended from heaven in droves and to the sounds of trumpets; how the shepherds came before dawn because they'd heard from the angels that salvation had come to Israel through a birth in a cave. Every word she spoke was stinging confirmation of what I knew in my heart and what I should have known with my whole being. His birth *was* attended by angels and heavenly powers, and trumpets and great lights in the sky. He *was* worshiped by wise foreign kings and surrounded by riches and wealth. He *was* adored by the common folk, known and beloved from the first moment.

As Mary spoke, I was confronted with the truth about myself. These past days can only condemn me: I chose to be a Pharisee before a disciple. That, while bowed at Mary's feet, I finally understood and accepted *who Jesus was* is of little consolation now; I am too late. Too late to save him. Too late to aggressively fight the intention of the high priest. Too late to use all my money and influence with the Jewish and Roman leaders to stop this travesty.

But it is more than guilt, more even than the love I bore Jesus, that has me staggering under the weight of these hundred pounds of burial oblations. I have squandered so much more than my dignity, my reputation. I have lost the chance to follow Jesus by day, in the light, for all to see. It is too late for me to devote every moment of my time to listening to his every word, to learning what God wants from us. Instead of debating Jesus' intention in the Sanhedrin, I could have been hearing his teachings. Instead of worrying about the politics of Rome's influence in Jerusalem, I could have been among the crowds that were blessed to listen to him.

I arrive at the place where Mary, so composed and generous with me this morning, now sways in the mud with Jesus' body in her arms. I nod to Joseph, my friend and colleague, and he relieves me of the burden of aloes and myrrh. Joseph has provided the tomb; I have brought the anointing; neither of us did enough to stop this. And we both know it, meeting each other's eyes only briefly before looking away.

I go to Mary, hoping to comfort her as she tried to comfort me, but I can see there is nothing I can do for her. Who could help her now? I kneel beside her helplessly until Jesus' head falls back on her arm, and I see the cruel thorns still tangled in the sweat-salted, knotted hair. Instinctively, for once not thinking of my dignity, I reach out and untangle the thorn crown from his hair. I am strangely gentle, as though tearing the hair could hurt him now. Yet, I feel that I must be careful not to harm Jesus even more, that somehow he will know of my tenderness in this terrible task. By the time I have the thorns loosened, my own fingers are pricked and bleeding, and I take bitter pleasure in this.

I fling the twisted thorns aside and cradle the precious

head. My eyes close in sorrow, and I think of all the simple and extraordinary teachings that came from this mind, the expressions I'd seen on this face, the words from this mouth. How could I ever have doubted that this was the Messiah? I lean my head down upon his in grief, as though I could once again have access to all the brilliance that resides there.

*I am transported back to our first meeting.* It is just after twilight, and the disciples are staying with him in a small dwelling offered by another follower. They are all inside, reclining before a sparse evening meal, and I can hear excited talk and laughter. I linger in the shadows, suddenly afraid to make myself known, afraid they will scorn my cowardice for coming only at night. But I have heard much about Jesus, and I am burning to meet him and see for myself. I think, secretly, that I will find there is nothing more here than a simple, well-meaning, ragged preacher who has captured the imagination of the people. Still, I find that now I am here, I don't know how to approach the group.

He must sense my lurking presence, for soon I see a solitary figure leave the dwelling and stroll out into the garden. He walks unhurriedly to where I stand, somehow able to see me in the darkness. I feel relieved and embarrassed all at once. What must he think of me, hiding like a child? When Jesus is close enough for me to see his features, my worst fears are confirmed. He is laughing at me! He makes no sound, but I can see the amusement and immediately bristle, knowing it is at my expense. I turn to leave without saying a word. But Jesus reaches out and firmly takes my arm, gesturing toward some large rocks where we may sit. I look closely, suspiciously, at his face again and see what I missed in my quick shame and anger. His silent laughter is joyful and knowing, communicating comprehension and welcome all at once. I follow Jesus to the rocks and we sit.

I am so earnest, so determined to make myself understood, and I run through my words, trying to demonstrate that I am no ruffian, no common Jew who will be quick to follow anyone who offers a few words of solace or revolution. I am simply interested in what he has to say. However, I can see instantly, even as I speak, that Jesus already knows me—and not just who I am among the leaders of Israel, but who I am as a man. Falling silent, I lean away, fearful that he sees things about me that even I don't know. When Jesus answers me, it is with a mixture of exasperation and affection that I am not accustomed to and certainly do not expect.

He tells me things that are unheard of in Israel, and yet he seems to have a knowledge of the prophets—their very spirits as much as their words!—that I have never encountered before. I am astonished when Jesus tells me that those who would belong to God must be born again in spirit, born from above, born in water, born like the wind, born, born, born! until I, an old man so far from birth that I can hardly remember my mother's face, have heard enough! I am confused, distressed, uncertain, and I cry, "How can these things be?"

He looks at me with those laughing, chiding eyes and shakes his head. *Are you a teacher of Israel and yet you do not understand these things? If I have told you about earthly things and you do not believe, how can you believe if I tell you about heavenly things?* [John 3:10, 12]

I am both stunned and strangely relieved to be admonished by this strong, rustic man. No one, outside my brother Pharisees, speaks to me this way; why then does it seem right to me? I understand abruptly that here, I am not the teacher. I am the student. There is nothing I can do here but ask questions and listen. I open my mind to his words as they flow like an unknown river, both refreshing and dangerous at the same time, into the night around us. He speaks of God's love, and the Son, and the Son of Man, who seem to be one and the same. It will be so long before I come to fully comprehend all his words.

And then I hear what I have forgotten in these evil days of his persecution and crucifixion. I feel I am both sitting beside him on that rock while also holding his wounded head next to mine when these words come back to me. *"And just as Moses lifted up the serpent in the wilderness, so must the Son of Man be lifted up, that whoever believes in him may have eternal life."* [John 3:14, 15]

*My eyes fly open and I look up into Mary's pale face.* She has stopped weeping and is looking at me intently. She is trying to understand why I have a look on my face of surprised joy mixed with such sorrow. I cannot help myself; I cry, "He knew! He knew this would happen! In his own way, he told me the first night we met: God told Moses to put a serpent on a cross and lift it up over the dying Israelites to save them. Jesus knew God would do the same with him for us. He does not blame me for allowing this to happen. I think he has already forgiven me."

Her smile is just the shadow of what it used to be, but she offers it to me nonetheless and inclines her head slightly to confirm what I have discovered. Yes, of course, Jesus knew. My guilt is useless, meaningless, a waste. I played the role I had to play. But now. Now I have a different role, and I am suddenly eager to take it up.

# REFLECTING *on the* STORY

What role do I have to play in Jesus' resurrection and plan? What is your role? What role do we play together, as a community of believers? These are not easy questions, but we can see from the gospels and the rest of the New Testament that Christ's followers were asking themselves—and each other—these questions from the start. Nicodemus brings burial ointments and spices not only because it is proper and traditional, but also because he feels grieved and maybe even guilty: he thinks he has let Jesus down. He cradles Jesus' head, remembering all the wise and amazing thoughts that came from the mind of his teacher. In the darkest, most doubt-filled moment of his mourning, Nicodemus thinks that all is lost and that he is at least partially to blame. He feels he hasn't risen to the challenge Jesus presented him with.

Well, who has? A few saints and martyrs, maybe, but most of us don't come close on a daily basis, in our busy lives, to rising to the challenge that is Jesus. We, perhaps, are more to blame than Nicodemus for our apathy because we have known from the beginning of our spiritual education *who Jesus was* and is. We don't need Nicodemus' "Aha!" moment.

Or do we?

Could it be that we've become too complacent about the Good Fridays of our lives because we know, sometimes vaguely and without giving it much thought, that Easter is right around the corner? There is a happy ending. Why spend too much time delving into our grief, our failings, ourselves, when we know that joy comes with the dawn?

But what do we lose by not closely examining ourselves as the body of Christ in the world? We have heard before that we must die and be buried with Jesus so that we can rise again. However, we tell ourselves, this is only a saying, a metaphor, not something we are really meant to do. Yet, to more fully experience Jesus' death, to imagine helping with his broken body, to place ourselves at Calvary and the nearby tomb, is to gain a greater knowledge of what was at stake. Sin and death and guilt were crucified that day. Nicodemus experiences a forgiveness because his sins, like ours, have been purged through the bloody death of Jesus.

For us to rise with Jesus, we must fully participate in that death, understanding—as well as our human limitations allow us—what it meant and what it requires of us. Nicodemus and the others who knew Jesus in the flesh were blessed to experience and hear Jesus face to face. Jesus directly confronted them with vivid and sometimes difficult challenges during his life on earth. But our challenges are in his death, resurrection, and teachings in the gospels.

For us to manifest Christ's body in the world, we must first go through the process Nicodemus underwent; we must face our own fears and guilt. If we are unwilling to let Jesus "work" on us, how are we to do his work on and for others? If we are crippled by apathy, holding on to sin, refusing to accept the Lord's forgiveness for ourselves or to forgive others, bound to worldly goods and wealth, judgmental, deliberately unloving… then we have to address these issues in ourselves.

Where in Jesus' body do we see apathy? Not in the muscles tightened and straining against the cross. Not in the willingness to make long and difficult journeys to help and teach others.

Where in Jesus' body do we see the hold of sin? Not in the pierced side from which cleansing blood and water flowed freely. Not in the challenge offered to those who would stone the adulteress to throw the stone if they were without sin.

Where in Jesus' body do we see a rejection of God's forgiveness? Not in the adjuration from the cross for the Father to forgive his killers. Not in the many miracles of healing that brought health and forgiveness into one's context, both gifts from God.

Where in Jesus' body do we see avid attachment to wealth and property? Not in the ragged whisper that gave Mary into John's care because there was no worldly inheritance for her. Not in the praise of Zacchaeus, who rejoiced to offer half of all his wealth to those in need.

Where in Jesus' body do we see judgment? Not in the gentle, suffering eyes that watched soldiers cast lots for bits of clothing. Not in the unwavering kindness to lepers and prostitutes and tax collectors, rejects of the world.

Where in Jesus' body do we see unlovingness? Not in the hands, open even around the jagged nails. Not in the raising of the rich ruler's daughter or the poor woman's son.

In the end, as we tell ourselves by way of comfort, we are only human. We can only do so much. We can only make so much progress. We can only meet so many of the Lord's challenges. We are not Jesus. All very true. But in our efforts and determination, we can be, must be, Nicodemus.

## PRAYER

*Nicodemus, your open mind and heart led you to return to Jesus again and again. Though you could not completely free*

*yourself of the fear of what others might think, you still under-*
*stood that the experience of Jesus is something that must not*
*be missed. Help me to fully experience Jesus through prayer,*
*the gospels, and by acting as his body in my world. Help me to*
*avoid "standing on my dignity" when I am called to prayer or*
*action. Show me how to dance and laugh and be a "clown" for*
*the risen God. Teach me to work diligently to free myself of any-*
*thing that may hold me back from listening to Christ's word or*
*doing Christ's work. Aid me in embracing the energy of the Holy*
*Spirit when I feel apathetic or overwhelmed. Protect me from*
*the temptations of complacency and selfishness and too much*
*grief. Do not let fear hamper me. Teach me to take my journey*
*with and toward Jesus one step at a time; and when the time*
*comes to run, give me the courage to run! Amen.*

## PRAYERFULLY ASK YOURSELF

1. Which of Jesus' teachings is most challenging to me, and why?

2. What can I do today to rise to the challenge of that teaching?

3. When we feel confused, as Nicodemus felt confused, by Jesus' words and expectations of us, what can we do to seek clarification? How can we more closely follow Jesus in those times?

## TAKE ACTION

Jesus may well been one of the most challenging historical figures to walk the earth. What he asked of us goes beyond what just about any other religious or secular leaders have asked of their followers. Jesus had the audacity to ask us to love each other! And not just our family, friends, and even that difficult neighbor, but everyone! For most people, Jesus' most confounding challenge comes down to this one: *"In everything do to others as you would have them do to you; for this is the law and the prophets"* (Matthew 7:12). Find an opportunity today to show love in some form to the most difficult person in your life. Obviously, this doesn't mean throwing your arms around your petty, passive-aggressive, stingy boss; covering the sour-faced clerk at your grocery store with kisses; or giving the neighbor who blares loud hard rock music a CD of hard rock's greatest hits. Even Jesus doesn't expect you to sprout a halo in one day. Nevertheless, do something kind, compassionate, or simply considerate for someone whom you find tough to get along with or even accept. Think of something—*any* thing— about your irritating boss that you admire, and then tell him or her in as sincere and non-fawning a way as you can manage. Thank the scowling clerk and offer to do your own bagging; leave with a sincere "God bless you!" Tell the head-banger next door that you've noticed how much she likes music, and invite her to accompany you to a free concert in a local park, on a beach, or in a church or a community hall. Remember that loving others is not expressed by a thought, but by an action.

## Five

# SALOME, MOTHER *of* JAMES *and* JOHN

*Then the mother of the sons of Zebedee came to him with*
*her sons, and kneeling before him, she asked a favor of*
*him. And he said, "What do you want?" She said to him,*
*"Declare that these two sons of mine will sit, one at your*
*right hand and one at your left, in your kingdom."*

**MATTHEW 20:20-21**

OH, WHAT HAVE I DONE? *WHAT HAVE I DONE?*

Is it *this* that I have asked for my sons to share? Is the abyss of sorrow I witness now in Mary to be my own? Will it be me who will crouch in the mud, holding the bloody, lifeless bodies of my sons, one after another? Is it *this* that I have asked for: that James and John will be tortured and die in agony as criminals, humiliated before the whole world?

I cannot keep myself still. Throughout this endless day, long before the gray dawn came, I have not been able to control my body. It moves of its own will, constantly, as if trying to escape me, trying to escape this scene of devastation, trying to escape the fate I have begged Jesus to grant my sons. It is as though my body cannot cope with what has happened, what is happening; and so it will not stay in one place. I have been walking, walking, back and forth, nowhere, for endless hours now, like a person who has lost her wits. I feel I must do something, but there is nothing to do, and so I pace and wave my arms, and tear at my hair and clothes, and mutter like a madwoman. I feel like I may burst from my own flesh.

I am accustomed to being busy. I am accustomed to action. I do not like to think too much about matters of the spirit. I do not study the Scripture; let the men do that. There is not much place for contemplation in my life. I have spent it cooking and cleaning, being the wife of a fisherman and the mother of fishermen. I can clean and bone fish and roast them with spices in so many different ways that you would think you were having a different meal every night. Once I understood that my sons would not turn back from Jesus no matter how I cried and their father shouted, I traveled with them as often as I could. I can make camp and start a good cooking fire. I can walk on my own for hours. I have made sure never to be a burden.

My sons say I have unlimited reserves of energy. Be that as it may, I have made myself useful. Most of those who follow Jesus do so because they are interested or fascinated or distressed by what he has to say. Not me. I follow Jesus because he won my sons, and they all need someone to take care of them. Really, they are hopeless when it comes to minding themselves, and Jesus is…was…the worst. I don't think he would have eaten one good meal on the road were it not for me. Although he pretended not to care much about food, I could tell that he enjoyed my meals. I would watch Jesus eat, waiting to catch his eye, and when I did, he always grinned at me like a young boy, hiding and showing pleasure all at once. John and James and the rest of them, they would devour a half-cooked, old goat if I put it in front of them, but Jesus? He was a challenge. Yet, I heard him ask more than once whether the night's meal was being prepared by me.

I think Mary is probably not much of a cook. Or at least she must not have been when Jesus was growing up, because at first he certainly seemed indifferent to food. It made me wonder. Not that I would ever criticize her. Knowing what she knew, well, she must have had other things on her mind when Jesus was young besides how to prepare a succulent lamb stew.

Just as I am attached to physical matters, Mary seemed always to be enmeshed in the things of the mind and spirit. As long as Jesus was comfortable and fed, she was never concerned about the excellence of the food. She was not bothered by the fact that when it came time to wash his clothes or prepare his meal, I always took over. At first I thought she would be upset, and I was a little intimidated by her, though I never showed it. But she seemed perfectly happy to have me oversee the day-to-day matters of our lives.

If I had been Jesus' mother, I would have fought off any woman who tried to assume the mantle of caring for his needs, but Mary would merely smile at me upon occasion to reassure me that she didn't mind. How could that be? I used to wonder, what was this kind of mother love that appeared untouched by the need to manage and direct? There were times when I thought that John and James would forget their names if I were not there to remind them, but I never once saw Mary instruct or cajole or direct her son, though John told me of a wedding in the early days where she told Jesus in no uncertain terms what to do, and he did it. But I never saw any of that in their relations.

It took me a long time to understand. Mary's mother love was different from that of other women. She did not coax, tease, push, or even argue with Jesus. I never once witnessed her remind him—or anyone, for that matter—how much she'd given up for him. Indeed, I seldom saw her approach Jesus at all; it was always him going to her. In the quiet moments, sometimes in the night or early morning, I would see Jesus approach her, and they would walk a ways together or sit comfortably beside each other. I am embarrassed to confess how often I secretly watched them, their heads inclined together; and though it horrifies me to admit it on this of all days, I would be touched by envy. With all the talking Jesus did with and to others, why did he always turn to her in these dim hours? Never to the apostles or my sons, certainly not to me, however much I longed for such confidences, and not even to poor Magdalene, who would have given her life for him.

Always, he would go to Mary. Sometimes, they would exchange few words, but when there was real talking to be done, it was Jesus who spoke. His lips would move, sometimes rapidly as I watched, though his voice was low. He would bend close to her as though making certain she could hear every word. Rarely did I see Mary respond, at least not with words. Occasionally, she would murmur a word or two, perhaps ask a question, but the comfort Jesus took in these encounters seemed to be more in her presence than in her counsel. Often I saw her place her powerful, slender hand upon his brow in a gesture so tender I would have to look away. Or she'd take his hand and gaze earnestly into his face as though providing comfort and relief with her very gaze.

She is consoling him, I realized one evening, watching them with my eyes half opened from where I should have been asleep. I'd thought back upon the day as I lay there observing them and remembered that Jesus had earlier healed a man with a ruined hand, earning the condemnation and fury of the members of the Sanhedrin who witnessed it. He had been hurt and angry at their reaction, though he must have known it was inevitable for them to reject a Sabbath healing. But they had wounded Jesus with their vivid rage, and I understood then that he'd gone to Mary with this pain. As I began to think back upon the various times I had witnessed them together like this, I realized that Jesus often sought her out in the hours or days after he'd been rejected or publicly despised.

It had never occurred to me until that moment on that strange Sabbath night that Jesus might have been hurt by the accusations and derision of the leaders and even some of the common Jews. He never acted distressed when it happened. He never retreated or apologized or showed any sign that they could touch him. But it was often after those encounters that Jesus would turn to Mary.

And why not? I asked myself that night, for the first time understanding what love there was between them. How could Jesus not be hurt by their fear and hatred in the face of his kindness and deeds of power? Was he not human? Was he not a man to be wounded as any man would be by the scorn and distrust of others? And why would Jesus not turn to Mary, the only one who comprehended what none of us fully understood until this detestable day? How could he turn to any of us, especially when none of us—neither I nor John nor Magdalene—would even allow ourselves to hear his prophecy of what would happen to him? Peter even forbade Jesus to speak of it! Why then would Jesus try to share such an immense sorrow and burden with us when we would not even acknowledge our own fearful premonitions?

And now that it has all come to pass as he knew it would, I stride back and forth uselessly through the mud, feeling small and foolish for doubting Mary's mother love. Though I try not to look upon them—Mary swaying inconsolate with Jesus clasped in her arms—my eyes of their own accord return again and again to their figures. Had I ever really believed this desolate woman was not a true mother? Had I ever been so blind as to doubt the quality of her love? Had I truly begrudged her the few hours when Jesus laid a full and weary head on her shoulder and whispered his fears and pain into her ready ear?

What had they cost Mary, those moments, those admissions, those piercing indications of what was to come? Putting aside, as if it were possible, this day, this moment…What agony must she have shared with Jesus during those earnest, quiet times in the soft darkness? Were they anything less than a preview of this day?

I had wanted to be her! I had wanted to have such a son who would confide in me and speak softly in my ear of his hopes and plans and thoughts of the future! I had wanted my sons to be like hers, to carry the mantle of leadership, of power!

In my pride and envy I had wanted it so badly that I had even asked for it.

Today I fear more than anything left to fear in this world that I will get it.

Finally, my legs will take me no further. My ability to move, to run, to hide behind motion, has failed me; I release a wail of remorse and collapse upon the ground before mother and son.

I no longer care what the others here think of me; each of us is trapped in our own pain. Though John is right here, whole in body if not in mind right now, I have already lost him. From the cross, Jesus gave Mary to him, and now, God forgive me, I am grateful for it. I will thank God if John never even glances at me again, as long as he is free from the cup I forced to his lips with my request of Jesus. And surely he will escape a death such as this, for Jesus would not have charged him with Mary's care if he, too, were to die on the cross. Yes, John's love as a son is a price I am willing to pay for his life; if only I could be sure that this ransom is true payment.

Magdalene has already anointed Jesus' feet with the jar of ointment I set beside her in my driven wanderings. She looks as though this has won her a measure of peace, but I have no hope of such an easy remission. I was mistaken about Magdalene, too; but then, I have been wrong about so many things. I had thought her unworthy of the disciples, a woman known for disease who could only damage our reputation, yet her love has been as strong as that shown by any of us, even including my sons. Of late I have come to accept her, but now, as I look at her sitting by Jesus' feet as she so often did, I almost envy her. She has nothing left to lose. She has not bargained away the lives of her sons as the price for foolish ambition.

There is nothing I can do! But doing is what I have lived for, and so slowly I take off my damp cloak, and, rising to my knees, I prepare to wipe the crusted blood left upon Jesus' back from the scourging early this morning. Pilate ordered it thinking to satisfy the mob's lust for blood, but it was not enough. The slashes are deep, and I can see that the Roman soldiers who wielded the whip held nothing back. My hand trembles as I reach for the angry marks, and when I touch the torn flesh, my eyes close in a spasm, and I am returned to the last time I knelt before him.

*It is a glorious day with the sun hot and bright upon us.* We have come to rest in the early evening, and I have started the meal, scolding the young disciples who are my helpers for not bringing me enough spices. They have no idea how to keep things running smoothly, these young ones. I pause to glance over to where Jesus is sitting, back against a cedar tree, talking to the twelve who are closest to him, the ones called apostles. I am openly proud that John and James were the first among them. I made no effort to conceal this; after all is said and done, haven't my sons given up everything for Jesus? Haven't I given up everything to be with them?

I cannot hear what Jesus is saying to them now, and I remember how soft his voice has always been, even on that first day when he stopped by the boats where my sons were working on our nets while my husband haggled for a good price on the night's catch. I couldn't hear Jesus that day either, but before I knew what was happening, my sons had risen and were leaving with him. We didn't know what was happening, my husband and I, but I followed closely enough to hear Jesus speaking to them of matters that seemed to me to be impossible. Yet one look into the faces of my boys and I knew Jesus had won them with that strong-and-gentle voice and those strange, incomprehensible words. John's eyes were shining, and it was as though he couldn't even see me following, trying to get their attention. Neither John nor James heard Zebedee, their father, shouting after them, or, if they heard, they paid no attention. Before we had gone even a short distance from the shore, I knew that if I didn't want to lose my sons entirely, I would have to go with them.

And so I did, which is why I am here today, working while Jesus teaches them, trying to maintain some kind of order, to keep them all clean and well-fed. This is no small enterprise. As I watch Jesus speaking intently with the apostles, John and James particularly hanging upon every word, I feel a small flame within my body. Just look at my boys there, reclining nearest to Jesus, listening most attentively. My heart swells with pride, and something else. I have come to believe what Jesus says, but that doesn't mean I and my sons shouldn't have some special part in his plan. Has any other mother given *both* her sons, her only sons, to Jesus' work? Yes, yes, Peter and Andrew's mother, but she already had a daughter-in-law and a home. Has any other wife left her husband, angry, confused, and abandoned by his own sons, for weeks at a time to care for another man, another family that is not even of her blood? Have any of these other apostles left their parents with no remaining children at home to provide for a future, security, grandchildren? These thoughts gnaw at me.

I wait, for although I am not quiet, I am also not foolish. When the others are at their dinner and Jesus is eating the fine spiced lentils I have prepared, I unceremoniously pull my sons from their own food and herd them over to Jesus. Mary is with him, but they are not talking, so I do not hesitate. Jesus looks at me warily, with a small, sad smile. His eyes, usually warm with humor when regarding me, are now dark and deep and unreadable. I try to take no notice of this. Pushing my sons forward and a little to the side, I fall to my knees before Jesus and bow my head.

Oh, what false humility!

I hear Mary sigh softly, but I have come this far and I be-lieve myself to be in the right. "Lord," I say, surprised at my own bold voice, "I have a favor to ask." Jesus, with that same strange, knowing sadness, bids me to ask, and I do. I know that he will rule the kingdom of God one day, and I want John and James to be seated right beside him in that heavenly glory. I believe they deserve this, though they have not asked for it. I believe *I* deserve this, and, of course, Zebedee, too. It will be all we will have.

Jesus' eyes close for a moment as if in a spasm of pain. He keeps them closed while answering me in a voice raw with an emotion I cannot understand, *"You do not know what you are asking."* [Matthew 20:22]

Suddenly, I am afraid, even ashamed. I start to retreat, confused by what is happening, but it is too late. Suddenly, those intense eyes open. With great grief, Jesus stares at my sons for a long moment. He ignores me now and asks them, *"Are you able to drink the cup that I am about to drink?"*

Fear and uncertainty overwhelm me, and I half-turn to the boys to warn them, to protect them against what I now know is my foolish blunder. But they are certain. They are pleased with what I have asked, though they would have never dared ask it themselves. They both stand tall, beaming at Jesus, and before I can stop them, they reply, *"We are able."*

I cannot speak; I cannot breathe; but nothing will halt what I have set in motion. Jesus looks away and nods slowly, and when I see the tears glowing in those eyes, my heart stops. When Jesus speaks, I know it is as much to me as it is to John and James. *"You will indeed drink my cup, but to sit at my right and at my left, this is not mine to grant, but it is for those for whom it has been prepared by my Father."* [Matthew 20:23]

By now, the others have noticed that something unusual is happening; they do not often see me on my knees. They hurry over, and in a few moments they understand what has gone on between us. The other ten apostles are, of course, furious. Not, I tell myself numbly, because they don't want to be first with Jesus themselves, but because they have no mother here to ask for them. A moment ago, this would have given me vain pleasure; now it means nothing as I listen fearfully to what Jesus tells them all. *"Whoever wishes to be great among you must be your servant, and whoever wishes to be first among you must be your slave; just as the Son of Man came not to be served, but to serve, and to give his life a ransom for many."* [Matthew 20:26-28]

I shiver with a chill that is nowhere in this warm night and, bowing my head, tell myself, You sought to make them princes but have only made them slaves.

*Will this be the end I won for them*? I wonder, as I gently wipe the blood and grime from Jesus' torn back and shoulders. Shortly we will bind the body in the burial clothes with the aloe and spices that Nicodemus has carried here himself. Will I be present to do this for my own sons if they follow their Lord to this pass? If I am not, who will give them this small mercy? Surely there will be someone?

I grow calmer as I help to prepare Jesus' body, taking him gently from Mary, who seems to understand that no amount of holding her son will keep him with her—a lesson I realize now that she must have learned long ago. I am busy now, caring for him in death as I did in life. I think of the words he spoke so painfully to me, *You do not know what you are asking*, and to my sons, *You will indeed drink my cup.*

I suddenly understand that this was Jesus' last gift to me! With those words he absolved me of my sin of pride! He knew that one day, this day, I would feel the unbearable burden of guilt, and so he provided me with the words that would free me from blame. I *did not* know what I was asking, and the cup had *already* been prepared for John and James to drink long before I fell proudly to my knees before Jesus.

## REFLECTING *on the* STORY

"Be careful what you ask for!" It's a warning that may well have had its origins with Salome's request to Jesus, born of ambition for her two sons. Most of us, like Salome, have learned the hard way about wishing and asking for things that may not be what we think they are. Without fully understanding Jesus' mission and purpose, Salome asked for John and James to share in the Lord's glory, not even thinking that they'd first have to share in unimaginable suffering and pain. It wasn't that she hadn't been warned. By the time she made this request, Jesus had already predicted his bloody, ignominious death several times. But like all of us, Salome only heard what she wanted to hear. And she only wanted the good part: the glory, the praise, the honor, the joy.

Sound familiar?

As it was, history notes that her son James was the first apostle to be martyred when he was beheaded at the order of Herod in the year 44 AD. Christian legends tell us that her second son, the "beloved" apostle John, though believed to have lived to a very old age, outliving the other 11 apostles, was nonetheless hunted and suffered greatly. One legend suggests that at one point John was dragged to Rome in chains and thrown into a vat of boiling oil by the Emperor Domitian in an effort to quell the early Christian church. When John emerged from this torment miraculously unhurt, members of the church were strengthened. Both of Salome's sons, the men Jesus had nicknamed "sons of thunder" because of their energy and dedication, became the selfless servants Jesus told them they must be in order to successfully follow him.

Did Salome get her wish? Did she get what she asked for?

When we forget to "be careful what you ask for," it seems that God has a way of shaping the answer so that we get what we need but not necessarily precisely what we think we want. Did Salome's sons end up sitting at Jesus' right and left hands? Who cares? What they did do, thanks to God's grace and the gift of the Holy Spirit, was to pour out over the whole world a firm foundation for all who would follow Christ. They became the bedrock of Christianity.

How often do we ask for something, only later to realize it was the last thing we needed, or that receiving our wish might well have done us spiritual, emotional, or even physical harm? We need to be very thoughtful about when and how we pray for things like more wealth, a better job, a new house. If we become financially richer, does that mean someone else might become poorer? Might someone have to suffer with less if we have more? If we have greater wealth, will we use it for our own true good and the good of others?

What about that promotion we've been praying for? If we

get it, does that mean someone else at work who may need it more will be passed over or even let go? Will a colleague in competition with us be unable to deal with missing out on this promotion or job, resulting in a loss of self-confidence and perhaps even depression? And say we get the OK on the mortgage for that elegant new house we've been praying for. Do we really require that much more space? Or will we just fill it with things we don't necessarily need and probably can't afford? Will a new house result in us having more possessions, more to tie us down, more to distract us from doing the work God asks of us? Will we be able to afford that shiny new mortgage down the road if the economy doesn't recover or we lose a job? Could our dream house become our future nightmare?

Naturally, we don't think of such things when we have a burning desire for something. We only see the possible good that may result from getting our wish. We want what we want! That is simply human nature. However, God knows not only what we need (which may, in fact, be opposed to what we want), but also what is necessary for us to manifest Jesus in our world. God sees the whole picture. For example, if we lose a promotion to a colleague, it may be because God knows that the colleague would have gone into a downward spiral without the promotion. Perhaps God also knows that, with a little extra time on our hands from not receiving the promotion, we may choose to spend more time with our children, volunteer at a soup kitchen, devote extra time to prayer, or serve on a church committee. In that way we end up getting not what we asked for, but what God knows is better for us and for the world. Through an initial disappointment, God can lead us to better fulfill his will.

How can we more fully cooperate in God's plan when it

comes to praying for what we want? Is there a way we can, as Paul puts it, run God's good race, without having to be dragged, kicking and screaming and full of disappointment, to the starting line? *How* we pray for our desires can make a small but important difference. We can ask God for what we want, certainly, while also acknowledging in our prayer that God knows what is best for us. Adding the simple, but sincere, words: "Lord, please grant me this if it be your will for me, and if it is not, show me your will and lead me to do it."

Another way we can cooperate in God's plan for us to manifest Jesus in our world is to pray for something most of us would never consider praying for: the opportunity to serve. Remember that after Salome makes her request, Jesus tells the rest of the apostles that whoever wants to be great and first among them must assume the burden of service and even slavery to others. Seemingly harsh words, which is why we self-centered humans need God's help and grace to become servants. We can ask God to show us ways to do his work. If we are "new" to service, we can ask God to help us start slowly and build our service "muscles" up to prepare for greater action. If we are already on the road to service, we can ask God to lead us to the next level and help us to accurately "know" ourselves and our abilities as we grow into the people God wants us to be.

## PRAYER

*Salome, you had the chance to do what I cannot: kneel directly before Jesus and ask for what you wanted. Help me to learn from your experience to be careful what I ask God for. Let me be thoughtful when I bring my wishes and desires before the Lord. Give me the patience and insight to consider how what I ask for may ultimately affect me, those around me, and God's world in general. Remind me to seek God's will before my own in both my prayers and my actions. Help me to learn from your example that acting for and on behalf of Jesus should be the greatest goal of my life. If I falter because of the world, teach me to seek out the light of the resurrection to illuminate my way. Let my "please, Lord, give me..." prayers be tempered by my "Your will be done" prayers. May I never forget the most important prayer: "Lord, how may I serve you?" Amen.*

## PRAYERFULLY ASK YOURSELF

1. When was the last time I prayed for something that I wanted or thought I needed without fully considering the potential consequences of getting what I asked for?

2. How can I more consistently ask God to show me his will for me and how to better serve as his representative in the world?

3. How have we, like Salome, felt driven to be "the best" or "the first" in our lives? How has our ambition impacted our lives and those in our lives?

## TAKE ACTION

Think of an aspect of your life in which you desire to be "first," to be the best, to win, to make great gains. Now, consider how you can be "last," as Jesus instructed, how you can serve others in that area of your life. For example, if you compete in or coach a sport, bring enough quartered oranges, Gatorade, or juice for the other team or competitors to the next game or gathering. If you want to be at the top of your class, spend time helping or tutoring a student who is struggling. If you have your eye on a new home or apartment, volunteer at a homeless shelter. If you've "earned" yourself the freedom for a nice, expensive vacation, spend time visiting someone in prison or in a hospital or rehab center before you leave. If you pride yourself on having the best garden or farm in your community, deliver flowers or produce to your less fortunate neighbors or a community food pantry. Take action to be "last" so you can truly experience what it is like to be "first" in the eyes of God.

# Six

# JOSEPH *of* ARIMATHEA

*When it was evening, there came a rich man from Arimathea, named Joseph, who was also a disciple of Jesus. He went to Pilate and asked for the body of Jesus; then Pilate ordered it to be given to him. So Joseph took the body and wrapped it in a clean linen cloth and laid it in his own new tomb, which he had hewn in the rock.* Matthew 27:57-60

I thought Pilate would ask for money, but he didn't. He knows I am rich; these Roman leaders make it a point to know who the wealthiest Jews are, and they have no trouble discovering where we reside and keep our wealth. Pontius Pilate knew well that since I had gone so far as to approach him directly, I would have been willing to pay any bribe to be given the body.

But he asked for nothing.

Normally this would make me very suspicious and worried. If a clever ruler like Pilate asks for nothing now, it is a sure sign he will ask for more than you can afford to give later. In any other circumstances I would be calculating what obscene "favor" he is already contemplating asking me in the near future. Or I would be adding up my savings, wondering how much he plans to demand for some Roman "improvement." One way or another, I've come to expect men like Pontius Pilate to always collect on the debts owed them.

Yet somehow, when I entered the place where Pilate agreed to meet me in cynical deference to my religious laws, I saw something in his face that made me understand he would be demanding no money, no debt, no future "favor." The sun- and wind-burned color in his face was bleached, and he looked sickly. Missing from the darting eyes was the usual sly arrogance, and his stentorian voice was muted as though, for the first time, he was actually aware that someone besides he might have something to say. I had come in upon him quietly and stood behind him. When he caught a glimpse of me, he started and his hand went to his sword, and it took a moment for him to hide the fear in his face and eyes. I had to hide my own surprise at seeing him so disconcerted.

"You sent a message that you want the body of Jesus of Nazareth?" he asked me without greeting me. This was another shock: not that he didn't greet me, for a man like Pilate thinks he owes courtesy to no Jew, but that he spoke first. It is Pilate's habit to skewer a supplicant—and just about everyone in Palestine is his supplicant—by remaining coldly silent as he superciliously observes the person before him. The result of this, of course, is that whoever comes before him dreads it and often loses courage. I had met with Pilate before, so I myself was prepared for this unnerving scrutiny, but it never came. Pilate was intent upon me, and when I didn't answer right away, he repeated his question with some urgency.

"You want this Prophet's body?"

"You think Jesus a Prophet?" The words were out before I knew what I was saying, and I recoiled inwardly, readying myself for his wrath. Once again, it did not come, and I was glad that I had not averted my eyes in fear, for Pilate just stared at me as if trying to understand my question.

He shook his head violently, trying to clear it, and snapped, "What do I know of prophets? It is you people who claim to have prophets. So then, you tell me, isn't Jesus one of them?"

I drew in a slow breath. For months now I had schooled myself to avoid speaking about Jesus. As soon as I understood how he was antagonizing the Sanhedrin and the Romans, deliberately, as I've come to believe, I began to realize that there could be only one end: the authorities would have to stop him. And so, while I did not withdraw myself from the Lord or his teachings—how I loved to hear Jesus speak!—I did not go about openly with the disciples. I learned not to talk of Jesus with my colleagues in the Sanhedrin, to avoid the topic in the council. I did not mention Jesus in my business dealings either, for it could do neither me nor him any good for our connection to be well-known.

Was I afraid? Of course I was afraid! I have a family and a number of business interests. I have servants who depend upon me for themselves and their families. I could not put all that in jeopardy. I reasoned that I could learn from and debate with Jesus in secret without putting my life and the lives of others at risk. I told myself that I needed to stay protected if I hoped to do Jesus and myself any good when the crisis came.

Well, the crisis has come. And I have helped no one.

So when Pilate asked me about Jesus, I felt immediately

inclined to retreat within myself as I had always done. Then I thought about why I had come to Pilate. There was nothing left to hide or save. I had failed myself and Jesus. I felt an unfamiliar sense of relief when I answered the procurator.

"I, too, thought at first that Jesus was a prophet," I told Pilate, whose eyes raked my face as I spoke. "As you say, my people have had many prophets, and we need one now more than ever. When I began to hear about 'this Jesus,' I told myself that perhaps Jesus was the prophet who would show us the way back into God's favor and out from under Rome's foot." I glanced at Pilate, but the fury I might have expected was absent; he merely waved his hand in annoyance, anxious that I continue.

"And so I went to hear Jesus myself, first hidden among the crowds who liked to listen to his stories and lessons, and then, alone whenever I could manage to meet with him. It was not easy, with my business and Jesus' travels, but we spent many an hour debating and talking. Gradually, without admitting it to myself, I began to believe Jesus was a prophet, yes, but much, much more."

Pilate's blanched skin was abruptly stained with fast-moving color, and he leaned toward me. "What do you mean by that?"

I gave him an appraising glance, and without ever losing sight of who he was and why I had come to him, I tried to explain. "You must understand, procurator, that when a man like me—a rich man, a member of the council, an elder of my people—considers the Messiah, I do not envision an uneducated traveling Rabbi covered with the dust and dirt of the road. My people have been taught to look to our Messiah for majesty and power and might. The Messiah, we have believed, will be so terrible and magnificent that we will hardly be able to look upon him.

"The Messiah of Israel's dreams and hopes does not look like Jesus of Nazareth.

"And yet I, a leader of my people and well-schooled in the Scripture and tradition of the Jews...yes I, a man of business possessing great wealth and influence...I came to believe that this Jesus of Nazareth was our Messiah."

Pilate's eyes widened. He watched me closely as he demanded urgently, "And now? Now? Do you believe Jesus is your Messiah now that I have had him crucified?"

He was not mocking me. He seemed determined, even desperate, to have my answer. I gave him none. Instead, I bowed my head and said with as much humility as I could summon, "Procurator, I have come for the body of Jesus. Will you grant this favor?"

My eyes averted, I heard Pilate hiss in frustration. He paced frantically for a moment and then called one of his servants, telling the man to go and see whether Jesus had died already. I knew my Lord had died, but said nothing. Our negotiations were at a critical juncture, and I did not wish to do anything to upset the balance against me. Pilate continued to walk back and forth, more like a caged animal than the governor of occupied nations, muttering.

Finally, he stopped before me and stood until I raised my eyes to his face. His was twisted in a mask of uncertainty and anger, a strange combination on such a man. "Your Jesus did not answer me, and now, you, too, refuse?" I stood before him silently, and a tremor of malice passed over his features. "If you want that body, you better speak, councilor of Arimathea!" he snarled.

I breathed deeply and looked directly into his eyes. I had one advantage. I had seen his fear and knew where it came from. He'd had much time to think about his encounter with Jesus, the words they'd exchanged, the way Jesus had made him feel. He'd heard about the procession to Golgotha, the screaming crowds, the weeping women. Every word that Jesus uttered from the cross had been relayed to Pilate, of that I had no doubt. The procurator knew that Jesus had forgiven those who tortured him. Pilate knew that Jesus had, at the last, called out to God, his Father. Pilate had experienced the violent change in the weather when Jesus died, though he now pretended not to be sure of the death. Pilate was having a day like no other in his experience, and he was afraid. I would use that.

"Procurator, respectfully, may I ask you one question?"

He gruffly raised his hand in assent. I asked softly, "Do you wish to be the one to deny Jesus a proper burial?"

I kept my eyes upon him and saw the terror flash in his hooded eyes, the swift intake of breath. He tried to recover, and, to his credit, a weaker man would not have been able to recall himself so rapidly. But he could only hold my gaze for a moment, and then he looked away. He began to stride from the room, and I panicked, thinking I'd lost my objective, but then he paused at the door. Without looking around, he spoke in a rough voice, "Take him! Go and take him off my hands!"

*I am a private man.* Keeping to myself and my family has kept me successful and wealthy. I do not choose to be overly social or let anyone know me well. I seek only to belong to one society: the kingdom of God. It seems strange to admit this to myself, but other than my friend Nicodemus, here with his head bowed beside Mary and Jesus, it was Jesus who knew me best. How could that be, that Jesus could know me better than my brethren on the council, better than my colleagues, better than my own sons? I can't say. I only know that I feel it to be true. The hours I spent listening to and arguing with Jesus were the only hours in my life when I felt like *myself*, when I didn't have to keep up an appearance or win a negotiation or make a point in the Sanhedrin, or provide an example to my servants and children. I told that to poor Nicodemus once, and he looked at me and smiled. "But, Joseph," he said, "isn't that the way it would be with God's Chosen One? That you could finally be yourself?"

His words astonished me at the time, but they lodged inside my heart, and soon I could not avoid the idea that Jesus, penniless and without any possessions to speak of, might be the Messiah. What was it that finally convinced me? What was that one thing or moment or miracle? What was it with any of us?

I look at Jesus' mother as she lets the others finally take the body from her embrace. When did Mary truly know the meaning of her son? Was it from the moment she knew of him in her womb? Or did Jesus perform some childish miracle like healing a dying goat or keeping a heavy cedar plank from falling upon Joseph in the carpenter's shop? By the time that moment came, was it already obvious for her? Was the event just a confirmation? What of John, this young man who reminds me so much of my second son? At what instant did he know that his teacher was so much more? Was it an imperceptible thing, like the light in Jesus' eyes when looking upon the apostles? Or did John need something more, like the time when Jesus allowed him to witness the raising of Jairus' daughter?

With Magdalene, who can know? Does she even remember the moment when she first knew Jesus? She was so ill when he found her; could the disease in her have recognized him? She will never say, even at this moment as she cradles the feet she's anointed now, again. And Salome? She has finally gone still, and in caring for the body seems to have worked away some of her pain. Does she even *care* whether Jesus is the Messiah? All she knows is service to him, and in that she may be better off than all of us. And look at this baffled centurion! He lumbers around us like an overgrown child at an adult's gathering. He doesn't know what to do or say, and still, in some way, he too knows. What about his commander? Does Pilate finally know now, too late, as he wrestles with his guilt and a fear he has never felt before?

How often have Nicodemus and I discussed when each of us really *knew*? And yet we never once talked to Jesus about it. We never once came right out and said it to Jesus. "Lord, it was this moment! Remember?" Or "Master, when you worked that miracle, I knew!" How many times have we tried to pinpoint the moment when the blinders came off and we realized that what we'd been searching for in Scripture was plainly in front of us? Did Jesus show us? Did he insist that we believe? Did he threaten to deny us our private access and debates unless we acknowledged him as the Messiah? Not once. And it was this constant acceptance, this patient tolerance, this slightly amused knowledge of us, that makes me miss Jesus so much now and that pierces me to my very soul.

The question that strangles me now as I watch them shifting the body from Mary's arms is simply this: Did Jesus know? Did he know that I believed? In all my efforts to protect myself, my family, my interests, even Jesus himself—or so I tried to tell myself—did I ever let him know that I believed in him?

Tears stand in my eyes, and I am embarrassed. I have not wept since I was a child. I don't remember weeping then, really, and yet here I stand with the expensive burial linens in my arms, my beautiful new tomb waiting over there, my readiness to do what is right, and crying like a child. For I have realized that everything I have done today by way of reparation—giving my costly new tomb hewn so solidly in the rock, buying these finest linens, risking my reputation and perhaps my life before Pilate—none of it will matter if I let Jesus die without knowing that I believed.

I cover my face with my hands and weep bitterly. There is no one here to notice; no one will care. In one way or another, we have all lost so much. Shaking, I sink to the ground, not thinking about my rich clothes, only taking care to hold the linens up out of the mud. Nicodemus stirs himself and comes to me. I can only cry and murmur, "I never told him. He didn't know," as my old friend, now my only friend, bends slowly down to me. We are old men, he and I; our bodies do not obey as they used to. Nicodemus listens to my broken ravings and then takes my hands from my face. He looks at me with the most sorrowful joy I have ever seen and says, "Certainly he knew. Haven't you understood yet, my old friend? He chose us. He knew everything about us.

"Now come, give me your beautiful cloths, and help us."

I rise, a little comforted, but still wracked with questions and sorrow. I wonder if I will ever find the peace Nicodemus has found. I approach and gaze upon the poor body. They have cleaned him as well as they can in this short time before the sacred Sabbath begins. He is anointed; Magdalene still holds his feet as we prepare to carry the body. This, at least, I can give him: my back and shoulders and arms and hands, these parts of me that have become all but ineffectual with so little use and increasing age. When is the last time the wealthy Joseph of Arimathea has lifted anything? When have these hands and arms done the work of a common man? When is the last time I have used my body as I did when I was young and building my fortune? When have I last used my body as Jesus used this one every day?

Yes, this at least I can give him. I bend and take Jesus in my arms to begin to bind the body with cloths, and my mind, clearer by the instant, takes me to a night during the past winter.

*I have come to Jesus this night with a warning.* He is disturbing too many important people. The council has all but turned against him, except for a few dissenters like Nicodemus and myself. This cold, dark night I am determined to teach my teacher. "You must stop inciting the people!" I say. "You must stop mocking the Pharisees and turning the Sadducees against you! You must stop drawing the attention of the brutal, bloodless Romans!" I tell Jesus all this, earnestly and sternly, a father to a clever but errant child. He listens silently, face in the shadows of the night. There is a long silence when I finish, and I can see the wispy clouds Jesus' steady breath makes in the chilly night. I am exasperated, and I protest: "Nicodemus and I are at our wit's end! You are deliberately provoking them, and soon even I will not be able to protect you."

He remains quiet. I shiver, but whether from the cold of the night or my fear for Jesus, I cannot say. He leans forward, and I sense the gentle, good-humored smile even before I see it. He tosses a few sticks into the fire and, when it flames up greedily, looks closely into my eyes, still with that sad, soundless, laughing smile. He pulls the rough, woven cloak from his shoulders and puts it over my beautiful robe, drawing it close to make certain I am warm. He smiles into my eyes. And I know. This is the moment I know.

*It is not I who has ever been able to protect Jesus*, but Jesus who has always protected me.

## REFLECTING *on the* STORY

What was it like for Joseph of Arimathea and the others to "discover" that Jesus was the Messiah? Even Pilate knew that Jesus was a transformative experience for him though he couldn't begin to understand how or why. We really can't know how they felt, because we were raised to recognize Jesus as the Messiah. We have not experienced that most marvelous and amazing of all the "Aha!" moments in life. For those who were with Jesus at the crucifixion and burial, was there actually an "Aha" moment, or was it a gradual understanding, a small warmth in the center of their being that grew and grew and grew until they were on fire with the knowledge? Unlike we, who were taught from the beginning to associate "Jesus" with "Messiah," the experience of realizing who Jesus was may well have been different for each of the first disciples. We know that Jesus did not, as we say today, "present" like the Messiah the Jews had been raised to expect. Just as we grow up knowing Jesus is the Savior, they grew up "knowing" the Messiah would look like something much different than a ragged, rugged preacher dressed in common clothes, who ate and drank and stayed with known sinners.

So, it must have been an incredible leap for men like Joseph to see the Messiah in Jesus. Even granting the tremendous charisma our Lord must have had, no one—not even Joseph and Nicodemus—knew enough about the details of his birth and life to be able to match the Scripture prophecies with the man. And, as far as we know, Jesus did not enlighten them as to the history of his birth and early life at that point. He could have made it a lot easier on them—and himself—by just demonstrating the evidence in their own Scripture. He didn't. It is almost as if Jesus wanted them to work for it. He wanted them to experience confusion and doubt and uncertainty. He wanted to shake the very foundations of their world. He knew that those who would have to carry on afterwards would need to be sure *within themselves*, regardless of prophecies and Scripture and the law, of who he was. They would need the confidence and courage that comes of carrying that knowledge within their own bodies and souls, not just in their rational minds.

In that way, we face the same challenges as those early disciples. Yes, we have the advantage of already knowing Jesus as the Messiah, but for us, too, it must go deeper than intellect. We have to avoid the complacency, or even the apathy, that can come when we think we "know" all about Jesus. For us, knowing our Savior must be more than reading Isaiah and seeing how he predicted Jesus in so many ways. Our faith must go beyond what we learned in our religious education classes or how we feel after a powerful homily. Indeed, we should strive for a faith that mirrors that awe and joy and surprise felt by the earliest disciples: a physical and emotional faith that does not rely only on intellectual knowledge.

If we are to manifest Christ's body in our world, we must feel Jesus in our very bodies. We must feel the warmth of his love and protection just as Joseph might have felt it when Jesus drew the cloak over him. Those who were with Jesus on Good Friday understood over the course of that devastating day that they would have to become his body—arms, legs, feet, face, heart—in the world in order to lay the foundation for his teachings. They did lay that foundation, and we are the beneficiaries of it. By the same token, we are charged with continuing to build the faith, first in ourselves and then in others.

All of this means that first we need to challenge ourselves. Just as Joseph and Nicodemus challenged themselves to truly believe in Jesus, not just as teacher and prophet, but as Messiah, we must task ourselves with following Jesus and doing the work he set for us. We face the same conflicts, the same obstacles, as did Joseph and Nicodemus and the other early disciples. We want to protect our reputations, our jobs, our possessions, our wealth. We don't want anyone to think we're crazy because of how we act as Jesus' body in the world. We don't want to over-extend our volunteer and church commitments lest they threaten our employment, family, leisure, and social lives. We don't want to have to forgo or give up—or, sometimes, even share—possessions that we've acquired. We want to have neat little lines and borders delineating every part of our lives: Jesus and Jesus' work go here; marriage and family there; work up there; social commitments down here; computer and television over there; recreation in that corner.

But, as Joseph discovered, it just doesn't work that way. Jesus blows away the boundaries. To follow Jesus most fully, we need to bring him into every aspect and component of our world. We can choose to allow Jesus to permeate every moment and act in our lives, even knowing that we may seem naive or foolish to others. That is a risk that Christians have to take, and it is by no means an easy one. It may require a shift in our priorities, a different way of behaving today while still in the same circumstances we were in yesterday.

A beautiful legend suggests the Joseph of Arimathea was so changed by the experience of Jesus Christ that he utterly transformed his own life. He left behind his riches, reputation, business, and religious interests and became a traveling evangelist for Jesus. He brought Jesus to many different nations, according to the legend, even so far as France and England. In Glastonbury, England, there was a thorn tree said to have sprung from Joseph's walking staff when he planted it before lying down to sleep. And while the Glastonbury Thorn, as the tree came to be known, blossomed richly in the spring with other plants and trees, it also bloomed in the dead of winter, right around or on Jesus' birthday.

It is a lovely image, not only of the gifts that Joseph brought to England through evangelization, but also of how faith can blossom even in the dreariness of winter. When the landscape of our faith feels dry, cold, and arid, we can plant ourselves firmly in the knowledge that doing the work of Jesus is transformational.

## PRAYER

*Joseph of Arimathea, I am like you in that sometimes I feel so tied to the things of this world. My job, my family, my reputation: sometimes I am overwhelmed by my worldly obligations. Inspire me to give my whole attention to Jesus and his teachings. Give me the courage to experience my own "Aha" moment of discovering Jesus as the Messiah every day. Show me how to let the joy of the resurrection shine through my life. Renew in me my commitment to follow Christ, even to Golgotha and beyond to the empty tomb and into the rest of my world. Help me to feel the amazement and wonder of the greatness of my God and to show that amazement and wonder to everyone I encounter. Amen.*

## PRAYERFULLY ASK YOURSELF

1. In what ways does my faith extend beyond my brain and into my spirit, heart, and body?

2. How do others perceive my faith in Jesus in how I move and what I choose to do with my body?

3. How have we failed to see—or to search for—the teacher Jesus in our lives because, like Nicodemus, we are afraid of the cost of acknowledging him? How can we better make Jesus our priority?

## TAKE ACTION

Consider your priorities. Now, reconsider them! Make an honest list of all the important aspects of your life, the things you spend at least an hour a day on. Sleep, food, work, spouse/family, housekeeping, social commitments, television, computer, phone, hobbies, traveling to and from all of these. Can you find Jesus anywhere on the list? Are there any spaces for praying, faith/inspirational reading, volunteering, parish committees, collecting canned goods for a food drive, working on a community association or board, visiting/helping the sick, meditating on God's gifts? If any of these are on the list, great: move them higher and give them a little more time. Perhaps, move into a category that you haven't yet experienced. If none of these are on the list, put one or two on to start. Make a commitment to Jesus and to yourself to maintain these items as daily priorities.

# Seven

# *The* CENTURION

*Now when the centurion and those with him, who were keeping watch over Jesus, saw the earthquake and what took place, they were terrified and said, "Truly this man was God's Son!"* MATTHEW 27:54

I HAVE SEEN MEN DIE BEFORE. MANY, MANY MEN. Some at my hand, some at my orders. Women and children, too, I am grieved to admit. Yes, I have witnessed things that no one should see, and I have done things that no one except a soldier could do and still consider himself human. I have done what I have done for Rome because someone in authority has given me orders and because I live to follow orders. Was I born cruel? I don't know. I used to hope not, but really, it has come to not matter to me. How could it? For me to consider my motives, my thoughts, whether I am more cruel than the next man, well, what purpose would such an examination serve? It could not make me better at what I am, and it could only make me weak. I am old now, but still strong. I am a citizen-soldier of Rome, and I didn't reach the rank of centurion by blanching in the face of cruelty.

In fact, there were times when I *was* the face of cruelty.

The worst? It was one of the first orders I followed nearly 30 years ago as a young soldier, and it haunted me for many years afterward. I thought I'd purged it, finally, from my mind, but just today for some reason I have been thinking of it again.

What made me return to this gruesome memory? I remember just the moment when it came back to me. I was walking beside this Jesus, who was struggling under the weight of the cross, weakened after losing so much blood during the flogging. These wretched Jerusalem streets are so narrow and rough, and the miserable crowd was pressing in on us, some wailing in sorrow, some mocking this Jesus every step of the way. A few of the dirty animals even spat at him. Mobs! They turn men feral; I've seen it enough to know. At one point during the short way to Golgotha, a small group of Jewish women were crying and carrying on, moaning about the pitiful state of this Jesus. He stopped, and, although it is my job to flog them along the way, I too was hemmed in by the crowd. And, if I am to be honest with myself, I was loathe to cause this one more suffering than he'd already endured and was about to experience. So I let him draw a breath. I thought, why not let the man enjoy the sympathy of these women? He surprised me, though, for it was not pity or comfort that he wanted At least not for himself.

*Jesus turned to them and said, "Daughters of Jerusalem, do not weep for me, but weep for yourselves and for your children. For the days are surely coming when they will say, 'Blessed are the barren, and the wombs that never bore, and the breasts that never nursed.' Then they will begin to say to the mountains, 'Fall on us'; and to the hills, 'Cover us.'"* [Luke 23:28-30]

He'd no sooner finished speaking to the women, who cried and carried on all the more because of these strange, dire words, than I was struck by that terrible memory I thought I'd forced from my mind years ago. It came upon me in all its blood-stained brutality, and I could almost hear the shrieks of those women more than 30 years past.

*I had been commanded to accompany Herod's guards* as they fulfilled one of that old lunatic's most perverted orders. He'd been delving into the Scriptures and prophecies of their holy books, and in his insane paranoia had come up with some prediction of a king who was to be born in Bethlehem. A Roman ruler would smile at such a tale, and maybe keep his eyes on Bethlehem. But Herod? This so-called king? This demented madman, who was as despised by the people he ruled as he was by the Romans who ruled him, decided to kill all the youngest boys in Bethlehem around the time this "king" was prophesied to be born. No trying to determine whether or how the prophecy had been fulfilled; no considering the impact on his subjects; no consulting with Rome; nothing but a brutal, impulsive, infuriated order that all boys were to be slaughtered. And I, as the youngest and newest of the Roman guard, was selected by my centurion to accompany Herod's soldiers.

It was, the cynical centurion told me then, my baptism by fire. "You might as well know what it is like to try to keep order among these desert people," he told me wearily. "Their so-called king is a deranged tyrant, and these people with their religion and prophets...how can anyone rule such a place, such a people? This place is Rome's nightmare. And what you see tonight will keep you yourself awake for many a night."

With those words he sent me off to guard Herod's guards.

He was right; it was a long time before I slept freely again
through the dark hours. I never lifted a finger that night, never
clenched my dagger, never even touched the scabbard where
my sword rested. But I have always felt it was the bloodiest
hours I've ever spent in the service of Rome. Herod had ordered his guard to kill all boys under the age of about two. But
no one stopped to ask the age of the child before killing him.
I won't say that Herod's men were any worse than most, but
most of them wanted more than anything to be finished with
this horror, and they moved as quickly as they could. They
barely stopped to see whether the child was male or female,
and I've often wondered if girls died that night as well. I know
many women were killed in those dark hours, for I saw their
eyes die after their screaming abated.

I saw babies snatched from their mothers' breasts. I saw
fathers cut down for coming between their young sons and the
guardsmen. I saw women who refused to give up their children
beaten senseless. I saw children, just a few months or years
older than those who were slaughtered, watching with eyes
widened in terror, thinking that they would be next. I wasn't
there long enough to see the relief and searing guilt that followed when they discovered they would be spared.

It was a night of blood and torch-fire and ghastly moans, a
night of inhuman cruelty. I know that Rome has been called
brutal, and I have seen many things since that made me silently
doubt my superiors, but I have never seen soldiers ordered
to turn on their own infants. I have always wondered: would
Roman soldiers have obeyed such an order if Caesar called for
all baby boys to be killed? Herod's men were more afraid of
him than they were of whatever judgment awaited them. As
we rode away from Bethlehem in desolate silence, I heard the

captain of Herod's guards, a man much the same age as I am now, though then I thought him ancient, mutter, "Will that satisfy the bloodthirsty vulture?" He spoke to no one in particular, and his voice was filled with grim disgust. I wondered at it then, as a young soldier with no blood on his hands: that a captain would say such a thing aloud. But in my road to the post of centurion, I have voiced enough of my own futile murmurings to understand.

*So, standing guard while this Jesus gasped out final breaths* on the cross today has not been my most difficult assignment. Actually, given all the commotion and the frenzied mob, it went a lot easier than I expected. I don't know why this crucifixion reminded me of that slaughter so many years past; perhaps it was because this Jesus was convicted by his own council and then brought to Pilate. Why should I have felt so uneasy when I was given my duties this morning? Many of Israel's rebels have been silenced in this manner. This should have been a routine day for me. But it wasn't. I have found it more than difficult to carry out my orders.

I have found it impossible. It has broken me.

I am not finishing this day the same man I was when I started it. I know now that all this time I have been serving the wrong emperor. This Jesus is God's Son, and realizing that has rendered my entire life before this day meaningless—no, not meaningless, but something much worse. I am like a child, but a child who has done more wrong than he can ever atone for.

Even now, as I watch these people around me, Jesus' people, I am jealous. Imagine this! Me, envious of Jews! An occupied people, a people who were meant to be crushed under the foot of Rome. So Rome thinks! These people will never be crushed, not by Rome, or any tyrant who comes after Rome. Caesar may have thought it entertaining to bring the young Egyptian queen home in a cage, but he has not reckoned with these people. They follow God.

The ones here who followed Jesus to this burial place must despise me. I know they must, but I cannot bring myself to leave them as they take down the body and care for it. I have been ordered to be here, yes, but that order ceased to matter hours ago. I am here now because I have to be here. Because I want to be here. Because, suddenly, I have no place else to go.

I prowl the periphery of the circle of sorrow these people have created, watching them, looking for clues about what I am supposed to do now. They ignore me, thinking I am still carrying out my orders. They don't care whether I am here or not. By executing this Jesus, Rome has done all it can do to hurt them, to destroy them, and they care nothing for me or anything I could do to them. Like the most dangerous enemies, they have nothing left to lose. Yet, in the past hour, I have seen each of these people move from utter despair—like that of the mothers whose children were slaughtered that night—to something else. I don't know what to call it. I can't name what I am seeing in them. Peace? Resolution? Determination? Yes, I think, all three, but something more. The faintest glimmer of hope? Could it be hope? What in this death could give them hope? I want to know, because I must have what they have. Otherwise, how do I go on? What do I do now?

I observe each of them carefully, searching for what it is that they know, realizing by now that there is nothing I can do to intrude on them; they act like I am nothing more than another shadow among them. I creep closer, as close as I dare. His mother: I thought her heart would be broken, but as she releases the body to the others, her movements are gentle, her eyes shining with something besides tears. How? How does a woman watch her son die in so excruciating a manner—and she did watch; she stood there every single second and never took her eyes off him—and yet come to such calm? I know she must be as old as I, but now she looks like the girl who bore him.

The other two women, the solitary one and the angry one— even they have changed before my very eyes. The solitary one is younger, but she bears herself like someone who has carried heavy burdens. When she sank to her knees beside Jesus' feet, I thought I would have to carry her away, insane. But now she finishes anointing his feet and rises of her own accord, stand-ing straighter than I'd seen her stand all day, for she, too, stayed bowed beneath the cross with the mother and the angry one. The angry one: she looked ready to kill me when I followed them to this place, and I think she'd have done it too, were her grief not stronger than her hatred. As it was, she paced in tight, angry circles through this mud, muttering to herself and staring daggers at me every time I came a little closer. Yet as soon as she kneeled to wash the body, she began to concentrate on her work; and now she is quiet, her eyes on the young man, her eyes seeing the future. The future that I cannot see.

The young man is her son; yet I see in her the recognition that Jesus' mother has supplanted her. A Roman matriarch would tear the hair out of any woman who attempted to re-place her in the eyes of her son, but this one glanced between her son and Jesus' mother with equal love. How can that be? And the young man? I thought it would kill him to wrench the nails out of Jesus' hands; I thought I would have to do it myself. But the young man did it, and now he seems utterly changed from the boy who stood at the foot of the cross looking like his whole life was collapsing. Now he takes those wounded hands firmly in his own strong grasp, preparing to carry Jesus to the tomb. The young man reminds me of a soldier who has returned from battle to find that he is still whole, to find that he is now a man and ready to shoulder the next task.

The two older men: they are older than me, I think, though it is clear that both have lived an easy life. They are wealthy Jews, dressed well, accustomed to wielding authority before Rome took most of it away from them. Still, it is obvious that in their world they command respect. Though I do not have what they have—and I am as aware as they of the irony that I, a mere soldier, have authority over them in their own nation—I feel I understand what I see in them. Like me, they feel guilty, and although I cannot know why, I recognize that this Jesus' death represents to them a personal failure. Are they related to this Jesus? Older brothers? Uncles, who did not keep him safe? I see that they are crushed not just by sorrow, but by a sense of complicity. Whether they deserve to feel that way or not, I cannot know.

What I do know is exactly how they feel.

But even as I watch them now—the man with the heavy weight of aloes and the man whose tomb this is—they are altered. The one with the aloes bent his aged head to Jesus as though in supplication, asking forgiveness. *How can one ask forgiveness from the dead*? I thought when he did it, but now he rises and appears...forgiven! And the other one, the one who was bold and powerful enough to go to Pontius Pilate and ask for Jesus' body: he is used to giving orders, but he seemed broken, unable to do more than carry those linens, as though hoping somehow clean cloths could undo what has been done. Even when he falls to the ground, he holds them aloft, but he must be too wise, too experienced, to think linens, no matter how fine, will change anything. Yet I witness a change. He begins to wrap the body, and color flows into his face. His halting, trembling movements become sure and strong. His bowed head rises, and I see a frail, broken old man become the leader he was meant to be. I see him smiling!

I feel the howl of desolation forming in my gut, filling my chest, rising into my throat; it is a real thing with substance that will choke me. I am utterly alone, divorced even from myself, knowing these people will never accept me and I can never go back. I know that if I open my mouth, it will pour forth, an endless, decimating noise that will destroy everything in its path including me, a discordant revelation of all the death and sorrow I've seen and caused. If it comes forth, the world will see what I've seen and know what I've done, and I will no longer be human. It is its own thing, and I have no power to stop it.

His mother looks up at me, and distress comes in to her eyes. She sees what is happening to me, and she is sorry for it. Swiftly she raises her hand and beckons me to join them. I am paralyzed, not daring to believe this, but, yes, she waves me over to them again. The thing in me releases me and then leaves me without a sound. In the breath I expel it is gone. I am so relieved; the tears come, and I remember the last time I cried. It was that night with all those children.

I take a few cautious steps toward them, and no one seems to mind or, really, to notice. Her eyes stay on me as the rest of them take up the body. When I am close enough, she motions, still without speaking, for me to help lift her son. I am instantly fearful and take a step back. No, I tell her with my eyes, you do not know who I am. She does not waver. Her gaze gently requires me. I stop retreating, but implore her to understand that I cannot. I shake my head, unable to speak, and I tell her with my eyes: you do not know who I am, what I have done.

Then she smiles a little and nods. Of course she knows who I am, what I have done. She has spent the day with me, watching me execute her son. I choke out a low groan, and the small sound releases me. I step forward, waiting for one of them, perhaps the angry one or her son, to warn me away or even strike me. I would welcome it! But they do not. The wealthy one, whose tomb this is, makes room for me. I know I am stronger than all of them put together and could carry this slender Jesus like a baby in my arms. Instead, I reach out tentatively to take on a small portion of the weight, putting my shoulder under his body. Abruptly I stagger under an impossible burden, feeling that I will fall to the ground, but the others sustain me, help me, and I close my eyes to find myself living the day over.

## I am at the flogging yard, overseeing the whipping

that Pilate has ordered for this Jesus. I watch, summoning my usual professional indifference, but already I feel something shifting in me. I wonder if I drank too much wine last night; lately I've not been able to sleep without it. I feel that same lack of balance that comes with drunkenness, but I know I am not drunk. I consider all this as the blows fall upon Jesus' back, and I come to realize that something is different. He is not begging for mercy, not crying out in pain, not cursing the flogger. Most of them under this sentence do at least one, or all, of these three, but this one does nothing. I peer at him, a bit more interested now. His face hangs down, and I see nothing but the bloody welts rising on the flesh of his back. He is thin, sinewy, and I know he is one of the ones who defy appearances. He is tougher than he looks. I sigh, hoping this Jesus will not give us any trouble. I already know that Pilate has been upset by the man and that there are likely to be riots over this. Just what I need.

The flogging ends, and my men drag him back to Pilate, who, for some reason, seems to want to release him. I know how it will end; I've heard the bloodthirsty crowd, seen the powerful high priest and the Sanhedrin leaders lurking around. But this, too, is something new: for the Jewish elders to ask Pilate to do their dirty work. I wonder where such an alliance will lead, and I think: no place good.

It goes as I knew it would. The mob screams for blood, stirred to ask for that murdering jackal Barabbas, and the Sanhedrin councilors remind Pilate of his duty to Caesar. I feel an unfamiliar twinge when Barabbas is released; it was I and my men who captured that murderer, and so I tell myself I am disgusted that it was all for naught. But I find myself glancing over at Jesus to see a reaction to the mob's choice. For someone already so brutalized and undefended, he is surprisingly calm and, though it seems impossible to me, dignified. This disturbs me. How can he so coolly watch Barabbas saunter into that mad throng; he is witnessing his own death sentence!

Now comes the part I really hate. Trying to get the prisoners though the narrow streets to Golgotha. The cross makes it even more difficult, since there is so little room to begin with. And this Jesus is already severely weakened by beatings and the flogging. This is going to be worse than most. Every time he stumbles and falls, I expect him to stay down, and I ready myself to order one of my men to lift the cross, but each time Jesus rises and carries it forward, staggering step by agonizing step. He meets the women, and I let them speak. We are

almost there. When he falls the third time, I find myself darting forward to take the cross off him, and then I catch myself.
What am I doing? I look around quickly to make sure no one
has seen my foolishness, but everyone is focused on Jesus,
who slowly, precariously, rises yet again. Some of my soldiers
look as shaken as I feel, and I strive to hide my dismay. I must
remain a good example for them.

By the time we strip and lay Jesus on the cross, I think I
almost see relief in the exhausted eyes, the skin around them
bruised and swollen. Oh, son of man, I think, as those eyes
lock on mine, you would not be relieved if you knew what
comes next. I swiftly break the gaze between us and harshly
order the nails to be pounded in. Though I turn away, I flinch
at the sharp cry of anguish when the nails penetrate flesh. How
many times before now have I heard that scream and ignored
it? Then why does this man's cry loosen my legs and make
me fear falling to my knees? A few moments pass, and I hear
words that chill me to my bones.

*"Father, forgive them; for they do not know what they are do-
ing."* [Luke 23:34]

He is hoisted up, and the wait begins. Normally, I would
leave now to make sure the crowd is under control, to report
back to Pilate, but I am unwilling to move. I tell myself that
there is danger from the mob here, requiring me by duty to
stay, but now everyone is subdued. It is one thing, I can tell
you, to demand a crucifixion and quite another to witness it.
The blood lust is down now in most of them, but there are
agents of Rome and the Sanhedrin here still trying to do damage to this Jesus' reputation, mocking him for all to hear.

*"You who would destroy the temple and rebuild it in three
days, save yourself!"* [Matthew 27:40]

*"He saved others; he cannot save himself. He is the King of Is-rael; let him come down from the cross now and we will believe in him!"* [Matthew 27:42]

I am suddenly enraged at these vultures, pecking at the eyes of the dying before the relief of death has come. I start to fly at them, intending to flay them and scatter them like vermin, but again, I catch myself. How will it look for the centurion to defend a condemned and rebellious Jew? Instead, I order my men to keep back all but the mother and her companions. One of my older soldiers gives me a strange look, but the younger ones are wide-eyed and distressed, eager to do what little they can to help this strange Jew who has already forgiven them for doing their duty. The vicious stragglers are driven back, and the wait resumes.

Has it ever taken so long for death to come? Of course it has; some of these hearty Jewish rabble-rousers hang on for the entire day. But the truth is that by the time noon comes, I am shaken and wrung out by this waiting. And yet, the thought of putting him out of his misery with my own sword shakes me so violently that bile comes into my mouth, and I stride away a distance to spit where no one can witness my failing courage.

As I return, compelled to be near the cross, the land turns dark. I have seen weather all over the world from Gaul to this desert place, but I have never seen the sky darken like this. I have seen the sun eclipsed and understand how the planets move, but this is not that. This is night in the middle of the day, and there is no earthly cause for it.

Except for this man.

Now the desire for a merciful death leaves me, for I wonder: if this is the world while he is alive on that cross, what will happen when he dies on it?

I can see my men are frightened, restless, and the older soldier who looked askance at me earlier now glances at me uncertainly, fearfully. I notice that those mocking him are gone, probably to hide in their fine homes or meet in their ornate council to discuss this latest turn of events. I wish them anguish; for they and Pilate are the ones who put me in this place, this position.

And we wait. His mother and the other two women and the young man do not leave him. Indeed, I can see that they are trying to breathe *for* him, as though they can make their lungs his lungs and their heartbeat his heartbeat. Except for the mother; she is holding her breath.

The sky, if anything, has grown more ominous; people are crying out fearfully, some beating their breasts. Too late now for your pathetic regrets, I think viciously; you should have thought of that long ago. And then comes that raw and ragged cry that I know will echo in my mind for as long as I live.

*"Eli, Eli, Lema Sabachthani?"* [Matthew 27:46]

My blood turns to ice, for even I know he is calling on God, the one he calls Father, the one who I suddenly know will bring Rome—and any other defiant, self-anointed empire—to its knees. I am filled with this terrifying revelation, and with the dawning realization that this Jesus is the Son of that very God. As I stand, rooted to the ground, Jesus dies.

*I manage to bear up under the implausibly massive burden of Jesus' slight body.* The others help me, knowing that I am new to this, that I am an infant in the knowledge of what they have known for some time. We lay the body down in the rich Jew's new tomb, and as I step back from the group, feeling unworthy to witness this farewell between them and their Lord, a soldier comes up to me. He has come directly from Pilate along with a small guard. "Their high priest has convinced Pilate to send a guard for the tomb," he tells me indifferently, adding with a derisive snort, "easy duty for me."

I want to shake him until the truth that is coursing through me overcomes him too, but I don't. I say only, "I will stay and watch with you."

I don't tell him that nothing in this known world could drive me away.

## REFLECTING *on the* STORY

The centurion is the first of us. He is the first Gentile from what is now known as the western world who is recorded as recognizing and declaring Jesus to be the Son of God. He is the first believer—in many ways, our ancestor in faith. Unlike all the others who were with Jesus on Good Friday, the centurion had no concept of Jesus and certainly no belief in him. The centurion, like any good, pagan Roman, would have believed in a pantheon of petty gods and goddesses, mirroring those of Greek culture. He would have thought the monotheistic Jews a strange and contrary people for their devotion to the one and only God. He simply would not have understood.

In a way, then, his conversion at the foot of the cross was

more spectacular in its scope than the faith of any of the others who had known and come to believe in Jesus through many acts and conversations and miracles and revelations. The centurion had no history that might have prepared him even for the possibility of a messiah, never mind a messiah who appeared as an impoverished, itinerant, and, finally, condemned preacher. It is likely that, until Good Friday, the centurion never even heard Jesus speak, so that the only words he heard from Jesus were the words uttered on the road to Calvary and from the cross.

What happens to the centurion is not just a change of heart, but the creation of a new heart altogether! Total conversion. From nothing comes something amazing and wonderful and, literally, beyond belief. We tend to believe that the first Gentile believers were called and nurtured by St. Paul. But the centurion was called and nurtured by Jesus and through his blood. We are all called to follow in the footsteps of this man, the first Gentile to comprehend the meaning of Jesus. We are all called to the kind of transformation that shakes us to our very bones, that forces us to understand that following Jesus means that our lives cannot remain the same. We cannot follow the pantheon of the modern-day gods of wealth, status, gluttony, technology. If we are to manifest Jesus' body in the world, every day must be a transformative day for us; every day we must experience the presence and teachings of Jesus all over again.

In her extraordinary, incandescent novel, *No One Is Here Except All of Us*, Ramona Ausubel creates a character called Lena, a young girl who agrees to help her small, isolated village invent a new world in prayers and words. As the other villagers wonder how to begin, Lena is most concerned about explaining their decision to start again to God. She asks, "What would God want from us, to prove our love?"

It is a question for all of us; indeed, it is a central question of our faith. Not "What can we do to earn God's love?" or "What can we do to earn heaven?" because there is nothing we can do to earn those gifts. They are a matter of God's grace. But "How can we show God our love?" is a different question. The answer is that we show God our love by the way we manifest him in our lives and to our world. We show our love by doing the work he has given us and following the words and example of Jesus. We show our love through a combination of prayer and action that, together, become the cornerstone of our daily living.

Like the centurion and all of those who were with Jesus at the cross and the tomb, we often feel that we are in the "Good Friday" of our lives. Our minds and hearts are filled with worries about finances, health, family matters, employment, and any number of the significant concerns that crowd and threaten to smother life. It seems sometimes that nothing will go right, no one will do what we need them to do, there is no light at the end of the tunnel. How, we wonder, are we to manifest Jesus when our lives are such a mess?

It is a matter of believing that not only is there a light at the *end* of the tunnel, but also a light *in* the tunnel, guiding us and comforting us, if only we realize it. That light is Jesus, and we don't have to learn how to manifest Jesus; we already know what to do. We know the commandments, we know Jesus' teachings, and we know how he distilled the entire body of law into the commandments to love God utterly and love our neighbors as ourselves.

It's not a matter of learning, it's a matter of letting. When we fully experience Christ, when we let him shine in the tunnel and through us, when we allow ourselves to be permeated with his Holy Spirit, we cannot help but show that to the world.

## PRAYER

*Lord Jesus, in the throes of an agonizing death, you converted the centurion...and the world. Thank you, Lord! Thank you for giving me the opportunity to share in this conversion. Though I have known you, I have not always been fully open to your Spirit and grace. Help me to embrace all that you offer me, Lord! Break the bonds of anything that holds me back from being part of you. Release me from the grip of idolatry, and help me avoid obsessions, possessiveness, and addictions. Remind me in the midst of my own Good Fridays that you are right here with me and that you rose for me, too. If the events and circumstances of my life turn my heart to stone, remove its weight from me, and give me a heart of love for you. Just as you put those who loved you together on that devastating day, reveal to me those in my life who will help me through challenging times. Renew my faith every day. Give me peace when I lie down to sleep and energy when I rise. Lift and strengthen me in all goodness. Help me to embrace your resurrection with all my heart and mind and spirit. Let the whole world see my love for you in all that I do. Amen.*

## PRAYERFULLY ASK YOURSELF

1. How much of my prayer time is spent considering what Jesus really wants of me? How often do I ask for guidance on this question?

2. The centurion's transformation in experiencing Jesus was stunning. How am I transformed by the death and resurrection of Jesus Christ?

3. How do we identify with the centurion in expressing our

awe at the majesty of Jesus? What evidence do we show the world of the fact that we belong to God?

## TAKE ACTION

What would God want from you, to prove your love? When the child Lena asked this question in Ramona Ausubel's novel, she might be asking it for all of us, for you. The villagers in the story learned to do a number of things to show God that they loved and glorified him. They wrote to God, offering their prayers and the stories of their lives. They shared their food and opened up their homes to those in need. They exchanged services with one another, depending upon each person's talents. Those with children shared their children with those who had none but yearned for them. They took care of the elders among them. They came together to worship God in a temple that they built for him. Simple things, but they did them consistently and commitedly and, sometimes, at great cost to themselves as individuals. Make a list of things you can do to show God that you love him. You may be surprised to discover that the things you can do to show God that you love him are the same things that show the world God's love.

# OTHER TITLES *by* MARCI ALBORGHETTI

## When Lightning Strikes Twice

This book explores the wide range of thoughts and feelings that come when a crisis returns. It examines how people in the grip of repeated tragedy experienced the event, faced their circumstances, learned to cope, and found their way to a stronger faith and deeper trust in God.

**152 PAGES | $12.95 | 978-1-58595-378-3**

## 12 Strong Women of God
*Biblical Models for Today*

Stories of women larger than life, yet who were vulnerable and in need of God's loving aid—these are the stories you'll find here. Both women and men who read these stories will recognize some of the challenges they face in their own lives. They can take courage from the example of the biblical heroines Marci writes about in such an insightful and easy-to-read style.

**136 PAGES | $12.95 | 978-1-58595-326-4**

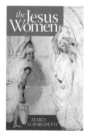

## The Jesus Women

These twelve extraordinary first-person narratives are from women who were contemporaries of Jesus Christ—and their stories make for great Lenten reading. Each woman experienced him in a unique way and each became a disciple in her own right. The stories are drawn from Scripture and invite a personal response through an "Active Meditation" and a series of pertinent reflection questions.

**136 PAGES | $14.95 | 978-1-58595-576-3**

TWENTY
THIRD
PUBLICATIONS

**1-800-321-0411**
WWW.23RDPUBLICATIONS.COM